BEHAVIORAL
PSYCHOLOGY
and
EDUCATIONAL
COUNSELING:

*An Overview of Selected Origins, Current
Research and the Application Implications
for the Academic and Career Counseling of
College Students*

BEHAVIORAL PSYCHOLOGY
and
EDUCATIONAL COUNSELING:

An Overview of Selected Origins, Current Research and the Application Implications for the Academic and Career Counseling of College Students

A Theoretical and Research-Based Guidance Manual for Career Counselors

by Nicholas Jewczyn

iUniverse, Inc.
New York   Bloomington

Behavioral Psychology and Educational Counseling:
An Overview of Selected Origins, Current Research and the Application
Implications for the Academic and Career Counseling of College Students

iUniverse books may be ordered through booksellers or by contacting:

*iUniverse
1663 Liberty Drive
Bloomington, IN 47403
www.iuniverse.com
1-800-Authors (1-800-288-4677)*

*ISBN: 978-1-4401-5942-8 (pbk)
ISBN: 978-1-4401-5941-1 (ebk)*

LCCN: 2009932964

Printed in the United States of America

iUniverse rev. date: 7/6/2009

DEDICATION

Twenty-five years ago, as a Pharmacist's Mate on a U.S. Navy Surgical Team overseas, I witnessed the extreme love that the Marines had for their Battalion Commander - they did not hesitate to shield him with their very bodies from fusillades of enemy gunfire. As a young adult in my early twenties, this seemed to be a most extraordinary event - that there could be no greater love of one human being for another, than to give one's life for theirs, or a cause. These days, I observe that I am gratified that I am fortunate to enjoy this sacrificial luxury every day as my wife makes her way into the marketplace to make my advancement and these books possible. This book is gratefully dedicated to my loving wife Cynthia.

ABSTRACT
Breadth

The Breadth demonstration consists of a 30-page scholarly paper that critically assesses Edward L. Thorndike's Theory of Connectionism as the foundation of *stimulus-response* Psychology's Theory of Behaviorism. The demonstration compares and contrasts John B. Watson's attempts, as the founder of the Behaviorist Theoretical School, to refute Edward L. Thorndike's Theory of Connectionism and performs a critical analysis of how these two theorists directly contributed to the formation of the Theory of Behaviorism as promulgated by the three, principal developers of Behaviorist Theory: B.F. Skinner, Edwin R. Guthrie, and Clark L. Hull. The demonstration evaluates the strengths and limitations of the tenets of Behaviorist Theory, as espoused by Behavioral Theorists B.F. Skinner, Edwin R. Guthrie, and Clark L. Hull, for the purpose of establishing how their cumulative, theoretical work has contributed to how humans learn and to the establishment of benchmarks concerning the framework of human personality.

ABSTRACT
Depth

The Depth component of this KAM is comprised of two parts. The first is an annotated bibliography of the 15 cited sources (i.e., refereed journal articles written in the past five years) around the topic objectives stated in the Breadth abstract. The second part of the Depth component consists of a research literature review essay of some 30 pages on this topic.

ABSTRACT
Application

The Application demonstration project comprises the authorship of the overall structure of how an assessment tool would be constructed and implemented to facilitate the career counseling of prospective business students who are in transition from High School to a Work Based Educational school or to a college freshman level set of courses. The Application component consists of a scholarly essay of about 30 pages concerning the structure of a prospective piece of assessment software and a critical evaluation of this assessment software based on the underlying principles espoused by the theorists in the Breadth component and the research in the Depth component of this KAM.

TABLE OF CONTENTS

APPLICATION

BREADTH
Introduction

Of the various schools of psychology that have evolved in the twentieth century, the behavioral school has made contributions to an evolving framework of how behavior could be more empirically and critically studied (Watson, 1924) and how the resultant learning could be used to foster improvements in teaching and learning (and as a by-product, counseling) in the public school system (Thorndike, 1932). Although Thorndike started his work earlier than Watson, they both performed critical research into behavior simultaneously at different locations and under different assumptions and circumstances. Edward L. Thorndike's theory of connectionism laid the foundations for what later became John B. Watson's theory of behaviorism. Although Watson (much later) attempted to refute Thorndike's connectionism, the primary sources indicated that both theories did overlap and that both Thorndike and Watson provided a conceptual basis for behavioral theory. The two theories shared a commonality and mutually reinforced one another's theoretical groundwork upon which the other theorists in the behavioral school later researched and published.

The foundational work of Thorndike and Watson developed and mutually reinforced the theoretical framework of behaviorism under the auspices of which the three principal developers of the behaviorist school of psychology researched and published: B.F. Skinner, Edwin R. Guthrie, and Clark L. Hull (Skinner, 1974; Hull, 1943; Smith & Guthrie, 1921). Each of these three researchers held their own particular belief system about behaviorism in general, but each specifically developed a particular form of behaviorism in theory and in practice.

This demonstration will compare and contrast Edward L. Thorndike's theory of connectionism with John B. Watson's theory of behaviorism and will present a critical analysis of how these two theorists directly contributed to the formation of the theory of behaviorism as it was later developed by its three principal developers: B.F. Skinner, Edwin R. Guthrie, and Clark L. Hull. This analysis will be accomplished with an evaluation of the strengths and limitations of the tenets of behaviorist theory espoused through an evaluation of connectionism, the foundation of behaviorism and behaviorism's theoretical development by the three principal school's developers. The primary purpose of this analysis is to establish the framework for learning itself, how humans learn and of course to expound upon the foundation of the benchmarks for the establishment of the framework for the study of human personality.

There will be three primary objectives for this analysis. First, Edward L. Thorndike's theory of connectionism will be analyzed as the foundation of *stimulus-response* psychology's theory of behaviorism with regard to the theory of connectionism's underlying principles and their eventual contribution to the formation of the theory of behaviorism. Second, although John B. Watson later attempted to refute connectionism, a foundational comparison and contrast of the two theories will lead to a critical analysis of how these two theorists directly contributed to the formation of the theory of behaviorism, as it was later promulgated by the three principal developers of behaviorism. Third, an evaluation of the strengths and limitations of the tenets of behaviorist theory will be provided, as espoused by behavioral theorists Skinner, Guthrie, and Hull, for the purpose of relating how all five theorists' cumulative, theoretical work has contributed to how humans learn and to the establishment of some benchmarks concerning the framework for the study of human personality.

Thorndike's Psychological Study Techniques

A principal technique employed by Thorndike was the observation of animals that had been placed in mechanical maze boxes so that he could observe their behavior in response to various contrived situations (Thorndike, 1932). The resulting behavior manifested in three basic ways. The first behavior that Thorndike noted was relatively random and it then gradually proceeded, by trial and error (gradually, the randomness of the behavior was eliminated), toward a correct response. Thus, the correct responses were eventually ingrained within the monkey or pig test animal and the incorrect responses were gradually eliminated. Thorndike concluded that

By and large, those connections which produce satisfying after-effects wax and those which produce discomfort wane. We have shown that the repeated occurrence of a connection, in and of itself, does produce learning in the form of increased strength of that connection, but that this strengthening is rather slow. (p. 170)

Thorndike forthrightly stated that a connection that leads to satisfaction persists. Further, when connections are repeated, they strengthen and lead to learning, albeit the progress of the strengthening may be slow.

The second main behavior noted was that test animals had to enact the correct behavior in order to learn it and that the animals had to have some reason to enact the response, or be compelled to perform that response. Thorndike (1932) maintained that there were thousands of instances where a particular connection strengthened others that were closely equal in strength and that the "after-effect" of that connection strengthened or weakened and accounted for "learning" itself (p. 172). This is significant since the effort expended was to promote learning in general. The fact that a connection, that was equal in strength to another, strengthened that neighboring connection and could account for learning in particular, builds upon Thorndike's thesis.

The third behavior result noted by Thorndike was that there was no real connection between an animal's behavior and the actual result. Sometimes, it was just coincidence. So, the coincidence of the behavior was noted to occur when the animal was prompted fortuitously by certain acts to obtain food; for example, by opening the mechanical maze box in order to escape captivity. In a discussion of Experiment 43, Thorndike (1932) remarked that experiments could reward or punish the test subjects and that the connections, which were satisfying, grew stronger. Then, the success curve rose quickly in contrast with experiments that had no right or wrong incidental to the connections (p. 178). Thorndike reasoned that the learning result had something to do with the order of events.

Thorndike believed in the relationship between sensory input and the resulting animal reactions. In comments regarding tests upon human subjects, Thorndike (1932) stated (with regard to sensory systems) that there was evidence (not conclusive) regarding the idea that "impressions" from one set of receptors could be affiliated with impressions from another set of receptors and that these impressions could then be "profitably connected" so that they would have a "somewhat stronger tendency to evoke the former" (pp. 362-363). This was tantamount to the discovery of foundational evidence that lead to the perception that learning was indeed taking place.

The Advent of Connectionism

As a result of this type of connection, "connectionism" came to be used to reference Thorndike's psychology method (Skinner, 1976). These connections, referenced by others in the original form of trial-and-error and other animal testing procedures, were viewed as the basis for *stimulus-response* learning psychology (Guthrie, 1921). In stating this fundamental, Thorndike (1932) maintained that it was an acceptable meaning that: there was a certain probability that a particular response (R1) would occur in conjunction with an associated stimulus (S1); there was a strength of association regarding the probability of the particular (R1) occurring associated with that certain (S1); and that, in humans, under "ordinary conditions" with that varying strength (between 0 and 1) approaching (or at) "1," these connections and associations between the (S1) and the (R1) "are sure to occur" as long as the person was "awake and attentive" (p. 19). This was singularly critical research that indicated, as a result of empirical data from experimentation on animals that continued with humans, that learning was taking place.

With regard to human subjects, Thorndike characterized learning by trial and error wherein the subjects were able to choose and connect in order to imprint proper responses and eliminate improper responses. For example, Thorndike (1932) noted in his "copying and dictation experiments" that the human subjects were admittedly satisfied with positive responses, as opposed to negative ones, and in the "listening experiments" the subjects were even more so satisfied although the subjects were not cognizant of that satisfaction during the experiment (p.109). These early experiment attempts by Thorndike were the initial introduction to this particular type of testing and to the use of a brand of scientific method involved with the actual, psychological experimentation.

The Law of Effect

By focusing upon the test subject's actions and accordingly, the resulting performance as opposed to whether the test was even unsuccessful or successful, Thorndike increasingly focused upon the "law of effect" (Thorndike, 1932). With regard to experiments concerning connection "after-effects," Thorndike explained these after-effects with a reference to the law of effect. For example, the closeness (of the "satisfying" or "annoying" nature) of the connection between a bond concerning stimulus and response could strengthen or weaken that connection and further affect the strength of that connection in direct variance to the intimacy or closeness of that connection (p. 176).

This law of effect learning was applied by Thorndike (1932), along with other facets of learning, to the learning that was occurring in schools. Not only were words used as stimuli to prompt coded response learning, but also Thorndike used "learning code substitution" to promote and foster learning among students and teachers in training. In the code substitution experiments upon students at Teacher's College, the subjects were divided into three groups. Thorndike found that the subjects in these three groups were "equated on the basis of the mean score" after only a single trial and that afterward each group continued to rehearse these code substitution tests with relation to "its own condition of distribution" (p. 539). This was a benchmark leap for the field of psychology in what would later be called "operant conditioning" (Skinner, 1976) because the latter condition was evidence of not only learning, but also of a sort of conditioning wherein the subjects developed "habits" (Hull, 1943). This was not only a benchmark in psychological research with regard to learning, but also an initial framework beginning for cognition and the development, through the acquisition of habits, of the formal study into the foundation of benchmarks of human personality.

Not only was the law of effect applied to humans, but also the system of "rewards and punishments" was further applied (in particular) toward the students' promotion through the academic system in public schools. Thorndike

(1932) summed up the law of effect accordingly, when he wrote that, "In the early statements of the Law of Effect, the influence of satisfying consequences of a connection in the way of strengthening it was paralleled by the influence of annoying consequences in the way of weakening it" (p. 276). A more literal interpretation of Thorndike's statement was that the reward, or the satisfying consequences with regard to the law of effect, could strengthen a connection's bond and was in inverse proportion to the weakening of an annoying bond's connection with relation to learning as a process!

An extension of the law of effect was the system involving rewards and punishments. Thorndike (1932) continued, and by default set a standard for learning and education in the school systems, with his basic explanation of this extension. He deduced that, within the psychological system, rewards and punishments both teach because of the reactions or responses produced in the subject. While the rewards strengthen and connect backward to the response, punishments do not always connect backward and may connect to something else. The "something" that the punishment connects back to may cause a shift and the "educative value depends on what this something else is." So, with regard to punishment, the connection could be weakened and some other connection would thus be strengthened and would then replace it "by strengthening some competing connection" (p. 277). By default, however, learning still took place in the subject and this method promoted the reward system for learning and positive habit formation in the test subject. This prompted the use of the reward system of teaching and learning in the public school system.

Thorndike's Animal and Human Subjects

The animal and human subject research was characterized by Thorndike (1932) as an 'either/or' proposition. He felt that the "person or animal" was coaxed by the after-effect of a negative situation, or a negative stimulus, to make one choice or another. Further, the choice that the subject would make was a choice that was very likely not to adhere to the original behavioral connection. The subject could either make an innate or adaptive response to the negative stimulus by avoidance (or leaving) or simply have some sort of "an idea or other awareness of the undesirability of such and such behavior" (pp. 311-312). Thorndike's ideas regarding human and animal learning were based upon the fact, from tests made upon animals and humans, that animal behavior was directly related to human behavior. In other words, "thinking" was not involved but rather learning arose as a result of a response to certain sets of induced circumstances and the learned response, by the animals or humans, depended upon that certain set of circumstances.

Enlarging upon animal and human learning, Thorndike (1932) insisted that "three very important sets of facts" govern this type of learning and they were "readiness, identifiability, and availability." Thorndike stated that "behavior and learning are influenced by the readiness or unreadiness of responses as well as by their strength" (p. 328). Thorndike eloquently described identifiability and its importance to connectionism. When the subject identified a particular set of circumstances, or even part of a set of circumstances, the subject could and usually would make a connection between one response and another response. So, responses to a particular situation were very much identified and these responses were distinguished by connection. The responses resulted in learning because it was easier "for the mind to grasp and retain than the original situations" (pp. 343-344). So, taken in context, this in actuality was learning by extrapolation.

These connections reinforced typical learning through the stated simplification that resulted from the inherent identifiability so that the organism (human or animal) could remember this simplistic scenario (thus, it "learned") and would be ready for future experiences. Availability, the third aspect of learning, was depicted in a very direct manner by Thorndike (1932) such that "other things being equal, connections are easy to form in proportion as the response is available, summonable, such that the person can have it or make it at will" (p. 345). Thorndike clearly stated that all three of the points above were important and should be present for the ease of these connections to occur that would then foster the induced learning to occur.

A Summary of Thorndike's Connectionism Theory

Thorndike's work in learning theory, through *stimulus-response* testing, resulted in the base theory known as connectionism (Skinner, 1976) and involved a variety of important points. From test trials on animal and human subjects, Thorndike realized that there were three behaviors that were incessantly repeated over vast periods of time in the test subjects examined. The first behavior was a relatively random, trial-and-error, eventual gravitation of the test subject toward a correct response. The second was the fact that the test subject had to enact the correct behavior in order to learn it and that the subjects had to have some reason to enact the response, or be compelled to perform that response. The third was that there was no real connection between behavior and the actual result and the coincidence of the behavior was noted to occur when the subject was prompted fortuitously by certain acts.

It is interesting to note that Thorndike (1932) did not exactly admit to the presence of consciousness directly, but referred to it in an offhand manner as a result of a discussion he made with regard to identifiability or availability that was secondary to a response, when he stated

> . . . presence of consciousness of what we are learning, or of ideas of the situation or the response, is rather a sign of a high degree of identifiability or availability than a force in itself. I suspect that if the adaptive or right response is available and is made to a situation which is identifiable, learning will be rapid, whether or not the individual has any ideas of the situation of the response, and regardless of any consciousness that he may have beyond what is a consequence of the identifiability and the availability in the case. (p. 350)

It is somewhat curious that Thorndike referred to consciousness in this offhand manner, thus by default admitting that consciousness did exist, but that he did not necessarily use this fact as a principle in his theory of connectionism.

Thorndike's ideas regarding human and animal learning were based upon the fact, from tests made upon animals and humans, that animal behavior was directly related to human behavior. In other words, "thinking" was not involved but rather learning arose as a result of a response to certain sets of induced circumstances and that the learned response, by the animals or humans, depended upon that certain set of circumstances involved. Thorndike's law of effect promoted an extension system involving rewards and punishments. Enlarging upon animal and human learning, Thorndike (1932) insisted that "three very important sets of facts" govern this type of learning and that they were readiness, identifiability, and availability (p. 328). The behaviors noted by Thorndike, as well as his set of standards concerning connections, formed the theory of connectionism. This theory framework became the pre-cursor upon which the behaviors noted were so expounded upon, that they later were to be characterized (by name) as the "Theory of Behavior" (Hull, 1943).

Watson as a Behaviorist

Watson's basis for psychology was that it was completely objective. Watson (1924) went so far as to describe a means of ordering this objectivity through the use of "word substitutes for objects" (p. 187). Watson set the over-riding tone for this psychological basis when he clearly stated that it was extremely important that objects in the surrounding environments were all named.

Further, words in and of themselves, were linked to other words and then to phrases and, if "the human being is properly organized," those eventual phrases could prompt the subject to describe virtually all operating activities. So, the words then acted as stimuli that prompted the responses, very similar to what occurred for the objects that the words were originally used for, to "serve as substitutes" (p. 187).

This objectivity was honed with decades of experimentation on animal test subjects and Watson (1924) later worked diligently to also apply his rigorous experimentation methodology to human test subjects in controlled laboratory settings. Watson synthesized this with, "Our studies on the formation of habits in both the human and animal realms have lacked theoretical guidance, nevertheless much information valuable for psychology has been obtained from them" (p. 25). The basis of Watson's "behaviorism" (p. 3) rested primarily upon two talking points: that behavior was empirical data for psychological study; and, that there was a lack of the existence of 'consciousness.'

Watson's Two Principal Viewpoints of Behaviorism

To set the tone for the first of these two viewpoints, that behavior was indeed the foundation for all raw data in psychology, Watson (1924) began with the idea that when man first came into being, there was a sub-set of reactions that could be called "man's *unlearned behavior.*" In that original sub-set of reactions, there was not what a psychologist would call an 'instinct.' From this, he deduced that the word 'instinct' was not in the sub-set of reactions and that there was no reason to really define any reaction as what was previously known as 'instinct.' Further, Watson maintained that the word 'instinct' should be removed from the vocabulary of biologists and psychologists. To continue, everything humans even referred to as an 'instinct' was acquired by training and was actually learned behavior and that it should be referred to as *"learned behavior"* (p. 74).

Watson (1924) moved this view forward with an important qualifier, with regard to the value of this observed behavior concerning its origin. He maintained that psychological studies allowed an appreciable comprehension of *"unlearned* and *learned* equipment of many species of animals."* He allowed that no observer, who monitored the activities of an adult test subject for a period of time, could actually pinpoint what rudimentary or minute part of a complicated behavior series was actually the result of learned or unlearned behavior (p. 87).

Watson (1924) confirmed that "the behaviorist's platform" was indeed that the raw data for psychological study was actually the behavior itself. He realized that the behavioral researcher should make only what could be actually observed into a proper, psychological study. He asked, and answered, a variety of rhetorical questions and he realized that the behavioral researcher could observe what test subjects said and did, in other words the subjects' behavior, and that *"saying* is doing - that is, *behaving.* Speaking overtly or to ourselves (thinking) is just as objective a type of behavior as baseball" (p. 6). By default, this means that thinking is indeed behavior. The fact that the behavior itself was the raw data for psychological study then lead to the second of two viewpoints: that there was a lack of the existence of 'consciousness.'

Watson (1924) was very clear about the fact that there was no room for consciousness in the field of behaviorism, when he stated

> consciousness...is the keynote of all psychologies today except behaviorism. It is a plain assumption just as unprovable, just as unapproachable, as the old concept of the soul. And to the behaviorist the two terms are essentially identical, so far as concerns their metaphysical implications. (p. 5)

With this statement, Watson detached the field of behaviorism from all other schools of psychology. He explicitly stated that his theory of behaviorism did not concern itself with the concept of consciousness and that this was a tenet of all of the other schools of thought in the field of psychology.

A Summary of Watson's Behaviorist Theory Viewpoints

Watson (1924) maintained that there were only two main viewpoints in behaviorism: that behavior was empirical data for psychological study; and that there was a lack of the existence of consciousness. He enlarged upon these two viewpoints, however, and maintained that learning in animals and humans was determined by a few simple, additional points. He used his conventional method of rhetorical questioning and made the psychologist consider whether the observable behavior could be stated in terms of stimulus and response. He broadly defined the range of stimuli as environmental factors that cause a physiological change (for example, chemical changes in skin tissue) in the test subject. Like Thorndike, Watson equated animal test subject behavior with the behavior of human test subjects, when he made a quantum leap with the statement that "by response we mean anything the animal does... and more highly organized activities such as building a skyscraper, drawing plans, having babies, writing books, and the like" (pp. 6-7). Watson reasoned that humans do think, whereas Thorndike did not give that concept much credence. Thorndike explained thought with a reference to some simple reactions to stimuli and Watson actually endorsed the idea that humans think and talked about this idea at some length. It is important to note that, like Thorndike (1932), Watson' s position very specifically stated that animal and human learning was related and was described by only a very few, principal points.

Watson's Four Foundations of Behaviorism

Beyond the two main viewpoints in behaviorism, Watson (1924) contended that there were four principal points that were the foundations of behaviorism and that they were essential to the behaviorist's argument. Watson asserted that the first of four points, essential to the behaviorist's position, was that behavior was essentially a group of responses and that natural science and its methods could profitably examine it. He contended that behaviorism was a science, similar to other natural sciences, and was very much a scientific cohort of the science of physiology. Watson actually mentioned that some researchers might not be able to separate physiology from the psychological framework of behaviorism. He further noted that the principal difference was actually not in the overall framework for study or the essentials, but in the way that hypotheses were categorized or clustered for that study (p. 11). This lead most naturally into the second of four points concerning behaviorists: the physiology of behavior.

Watson (1924) directed that behavior was constructed completely from physical movements and secretions within the body of the organism. He described his particular views, concerning the elements of physiology, but contended that behaviorism embraced basic physiology as a foundation and also included all of the "functioning of these parts." The behaviorist was really more interested in the complete organism and how it interfaced with its environment throughout the day and night (p.11). This simplistic reduction of behavior to rudimentary physiologic processes described the second of the four principal points regarding the behaviorist's position.

The third of four principal points, concerning the platform of the behaviorist's position, was that, given a pronounced, effective stimulus, there would instantly be a response and that given a response, there would regularly be some sort of stimulus. Watson (1924) was very clear about this when he definitively stated that, "It is the business of behavioristic psychology to be able to predict and to control human activity." In order to be able to accomplish this feat, he maintained that researchers needed to obtain raw, empirical data through scientific experimentation. Through the use of this methodology, he confirmed that it was indeed possible for the experienced, schooled, behavioral researcher to forecast a given response, relating to a given stimulus, and that the researcher could determine and state the precipitating stimulus for a given response. So, not only did behaviorism seek to scientifically determine that there was a *stimulus-response* relationship involved with observable behavior, but also, Watson contended that the purpose of behaviorism and behavioristic psychology was to predict and to control human activity (p. 11)!

The actual fourth, of four foundational points, has already been addressed in a general sense; that there was no room for consciousness in the field of behaviorism (previously, the second of two main viewpoints). However, in order to truly grasp the nature of this second of the two main viewpoints (the fourth general foundational point), Watson (1924) expounded upon this, as the fourth plank in "the behaviorist's platform." Watson, by explaining how it was regarded by the behaviorist and behaviorism in general, mentioned that, "Literally hundreds of thousands of printed pages have been published on the minute analysis of this intangible something called 'consciousness.' And how do we begin work upon it? Not by analyzing it as we would a chemical compound, or the way a plant grows." Watson contended that it was just not possible to objectively quantify, through scientific research or study, the concept of consciousness. There might be a certain sort of introspection contrived by psychological researchers to quantify consciousness, but there was no raw data or means of empirical study that the researcher could use to objectively study it. So, he reasoned that since there were as many opinions about consciousness as there were researchers, there was no palatable means available for its inclusion in serious, scientific study so he decided to exclude it completely (pp. 5-6).

When Watson expounded upon the second of the two main viewpoints of behaviorism and made this very straight-forward determination, the fourth of the four main planks of the behaviorism school of psychology, Watson discounted all other forms and schools of psychology. Since all other psychological schools of that time (demonstrated herein above) held that consciousness was integral to any psychological school (with the exception of the school of behaviorism), Watson set behaviorism apart from all other psychological schools by denying the existence of consciousness on the basis that it could not be scientifically studied.

An Analysis of Thorndike's Connectionism and Watson's Behaviorism

There are some similarities between the connectionism system of psychology put forth by Thorndike and the behaviorism framework put forth by Watson. The first behavior discussed by Thorndike was similar to the Watson (1924) theory of behaviorism in a very important way: the first basic behavior set of connections discussed by Thorndike was essentially synonymous with Watson's "frequency and recency basis" for behavior in general:

> Why is the time cut down, and why do move- ments not necessary to the solution gradually drop out of the series? This has been a hard prob- lem to solve because none of us, I believe, has ever simplified the problem enough to really bring experimental technique to bear upon it. I have

tried to explain on what we may call a *frequency* and *recency* basis, why the one movement finally persists whereas all the rest die away. (p. 165)

Where Watson differed from Thorndike was with reference to Thorndike's law of effect. The trial and error tenet of Thorndike disagreed with Watson's behaviorism on the general thought that there were many more incorrect responses made by a test animal on the path to the correct response than Watson believed was the case. Watson merely stated that, "The behaviorist claims that there is a response to every effective stimulus and that the response is immediate" (p. 14).

It is curious to note that Thorndike does not directly address the concept of personality, although he did perform considerable experimentation and found values that were indeed the precursors to the benchmarks of the scientific study of human personality. In contrast, Watson (1924) devoted an entire chapter to the subject of human personality and in summation stated:

In studying the personality of an individual - what he is good for, what he isn't good for and what isn't good for him - we must observe him as he carries out his daily complex activities; not just at this moment or that, but week in and week out, year in and year out, under stress, under temptation, under affluence and under poverty. In other words, in order to write up the personality, the "shop ticket," for an individual, we must call him in and put him through all the possible tests in the shop before we are in a position to know what kind of person - what kind of organic machine - he is. (p. 217)

This is *prima facie* evidence of the start of personality derivation (in the behaviorist school) through the proposal of the actual testing of human subjects. In a very direct way, Watson set into place the foundation of groundwork necessary for later psychologist developers of the behaviorist school of psychology to work with human subject testing in the field of personality. Although Thorndike set a firm bedrock precursor for Watson's behaviorist foundation for human personality study, Watson really advanced this study into a legitimate framework for scientific study. This would later significantly contribute to how humans learn and to the establishment of benchmarks concerning the framework for the study of human personality (Skinner, 1976).

With the exception of Thorndike's law of effect, the experimental techniques employed by Thorndike's use of connectionism and Watson's use of behaviorism were equally rigorous, with regard to scientific technique. Their uses were also very similar, with regard to *stimulus-response* psychology, when they both experimented on animal and human test subjects. Both Thorndike and Watson employed the principles of *stimulus-response* psychology and the associated techniques, Thorndike with his principles of connection and Watson with his frequency and recency, in order to explain the sort of imprinted responses that lead to learning in animal and human subjects. Another similarity, with regard to learning and behavior, was Watson's (1924) objectivity through the use of "word substitutes for objects" (p.

187), concerning human subject experimentation, and Thorndike's (1932) "learning code substitution" to promote and foster learning among students and teachers in training (p. 539). An important, major set of differences, between Watson and Thorndike as theorists, was the fact that Watson embraced the concepts of human personality and human thinking, whereas Thorndike did not. This set in place the early groundwork for Watson to much later start to dispute Thorndike's early work in psychology and testing.

Many similarities have already been analyzed with regard to Thorndike's connectionism and Watson's behaviorism. Evidence, of similarities between the two theories, has been presented and we can formalize such evidence through a repetition of the first breadth objective. The above analysis of Edward L. Thorndike's theory of connectionism as the foundation of *stimulus-response* psychology's theory of behaviorism with regard to the theory of connectionism's underlying principles and their eventual contribution to the formation of the theory of behaviorism, can be described by several commonalities, research techniques, and principles.

The commonalities employed by Thorndike and Watson were too numerous to have randomly occurred independently or by chance. Connectionism (Thorndike, 1932) antedated the theory of behaviorism (Watson, 1924) by several decades. The experiments shown by Thorndike occurred in the time-span when connectionism was generally accepted as the rigorous and scientific foundation of experimental research in psychology during the period of years from 1898 to 1930 (Thorndike, 1932). Watson started to publish papers on the topic of behaviorism in 1914, but formalized the theory of behaviorism in a published volume in 1924.

The research techniques in connectionism and behaviorism were both scientifically based, with regard to rigor and objectivity, as has already been shown. The responses given by the animal and human test subjects were given to be the objective result of behavior and the responses symbolized the test subjects' learning.

With the exception of the Watson (1924) pronouncement concerning consciousness, the methods of both theorists, as depicted in the underlying principles (as has already been demonstrated) concerning their manner of experimentation upon animal and human test subjects, their learning and response outcomes and the manner in which the results were outlined and published, were in many respects identical. Thorndike (1932) does mention consciousness in an offhand way, but does not give the idea much credence in his experiments, principles or theory of connectionism. Since Thorndike did not dwell upon the concept of consciousness, as all other schools of psychology had in that time period (Watson, 1924), this became a very important point of comparison of connectionism and behaviorism: the fact that consciousness was summarily dismissed by both Thorndike and Watson. A very large difference between the two theories was the suggestion by Watson (1924) to begin testing of human subjects to derive the shop ticket of human personality; a concept that Thorndike worked diligently to avoid completely.

Thorndike's (1932) commonalities, research techniques, and principles were enlarged upon in the behaviorist school of psychology founded by Watson

(1924) and behaviorism owed a great conceptual debt to the foundational research exhibited by Thorndike's work. In some respects, connectionism is more behavioral than even behaviorism itself (Guthrie, 1921), with regard to the objectivity exhibited by the research foundations of the behaviorist school of psychology. However, Watson (in later texts, which are not the subject of this study) went on to later dispute some of Thorndike's minor work by later attempting to refute Thorndike on some trivial, unrelated points of interest concerning research, methodology and results.

The Five Assumptions of Hull's Behaviorist Theory Framework

Hull will be examined from a variety of aspects concerning his particular views of the theory of behaviorism. Hull's framework, propositions and the contributions of his theory to behaviorism will be described in composite steps. Within the theory framework were five separate assumptions made by Hull that contributed to his theoretical framework of behaviorism.

First, Hull insisted upon a completely objective means of acquiring and reporting empirical or raw data. Hull (1943) insisted that "an ideally adequate theory even of so-called purposive behavior ought, therefore, to begin with colorless movement and mere receptor impulses" (p. 25). This agreed ideologically with Thorndike's connectionism and with Watson's behaviorism.

Hull's *stimulus-response* variables could be used to devise dependent and independent variables when forming the synthesis of research in psychology or in creating a working theory. This second assumption agreed with Watson's underlying tenets of behaviorism. More explicitly, Watson's view also was that with the stimulus, we can arrive at the response; given a response, we can suppose the original stimulus.

Learning (Hull, 1943) stemmed from a dedication to conditioned response postulates and a related form of *stimulus-response* foundations as the basis for learning (pp. 76-77). This third assumption was also addressed by Watson when he talked about this and asserted that it wasn't just Conditioned-Response postulates that accounted for learning. Further, Watson also failed to discuss the details of conditioning theory in any sort of an organized way (Skinner, 1976). Guthrie (1921) informally carried out research concerning the association postulates and how they related to static learning theory, but did not formalize that particular research modality.

Hull (1943) tried, as other behaviorists did, to compress all learning theory into *stimulus-response* terminology and show that all behaviorist postulates could be defined in terms of S-R terminology (p.188). This fourth assumption was very similar to Watson's version of behaviorism and was typical (Skinner, 1976) of the early behaviorists in general, where they trivialized other types of processes. These behaviorists strictly examined and relied upon objective, observable phenomena, such as S-R conditioning, and defined much of their research in objective terms arising from observable, S-R behavior (p.81).

Finally, Hull (1943) kept himself in the spirit of a fifth assumption because he operated inside the parameters of the general framework of behaviorists (p. 382-383). In order to effectively compare and contrast the behaviorists in general, a critical discussion of the four principal postulates of behaviorist theory (Watson, 1924) is an imperative inclusion to this discussion. A later analysis of these behaviorists will depend upon a conceptual and effective understanding of this behavioral theory platform for theory discussion, depth analysis, and later application.

Hull's Four Postulates of the Behaviorist School

Concerning the first postulate, Hull (1943) subscribed to the objective postulates of behaviorism (p. 25). Although Hull put himself into the school of behaviorism proper, he claimed that he was somewhat different (ideologically) because he had some slightly different views with regard to behaviorism in general (p. 398). Hull did not explicitly deny the existence of consciousness. Further, the concepts of consciousness and personality were not directly addressed in this work.

With regard to the second postulate, Hull's (1943) theory was based upon S-R raw data and these reduced from the environment and were not organism prescribed. He further stated that the environment provided commodities and that these commodities "mediated" needs. This mediation occurred only as long as the behavior sequences corresponded to the environmental commodity provided and that they needed to "synchronize" to the commodity's provision along "with the several phases of the environmental reactions" (p. 17). Hull advanced behavioral theory beyond the basics of objective observation to the use of "intervening" variables that allowed a more sophisticated interpretation of the observed phenomena and a more convoluted theoretical interpretation of the results (p.57).

Early behaviorists, such as Watson, were somewhat vague about the sort of intervening variables that Hull had introduced. So, where these variables might have been implied (such as "reflex connections") by Watson, Hull formalized them as a part of behaviorist theory and defined them with names such as "drive." The drive variable could combine with habit strength and increase the nature of the response to various stimuli - something that was only vaguely referred to in passing by other behaviorists. This is truly a main deviation from the central, more traditional behavioral theory that was originally analyzed herein (Watson, 1924; Guthrie, 1921).

Traditional psychologists had indiscriminantly applied the terms 'stimulus' and 'response' to a very broad range of raw data, but also to categories of such raw data (Thorndike, 1932). Hull was more exact about what, according to the definitions of the terms, actually qualified behaviors as something that could be identified by those terms. So, Hull came up with "stimulus equivalence" and (to a lesser extent) "response equivalence" as more precise indicators to precisely define the postulates of his work (Hull, 1943).

To explain the third postulate, Hull used conditioned response postulates with regard to learning. Hull used C-R postulates differently from the more traditional approach employed by classical behaviorists. The standard type of learning did not occur due to any form of conditioning (Hull, 1943) described by any traditional behaviorist, but more closely paralleled the predecessor model proposed by Thorndike (p. 165). Hull reinforced Thorndike's theory of connectionism by reinforcing Thorndike's position on the law of effect with Hull's own "positive association" that relied upon the "reinforcing state of affairs" to make the postulate functional (p. 78). Hull's reliance for functionality of reinforcement, predicated upon association (with relation to Watson's law of recency), was synonymous with Thorndike's position regarding his postulated law of effect (p. 135).

Early behaviorists used C-R postulates with regard to concrete explanations, but made little attempt to integrate these comments into an overall theoretical framework (Guthrie, 1921). Hull (1943), on the other hand, used these C-R postulates decisively in the objective sense and also integrated these C-R postulates into the framework of his theoretical interpretation of behaviorism (p. 382).

Early behaviorists, and "would-be" behaviorists (Guthrie, 1921; Thorndike, 1932), were also content to apply C-R postulates in a subjective or qualitative way with regard to research. Hull (1943) made it a point to specifically apply C-R postulates in an objective, quantitative way to his research (p. 30). Hull actually inserted the experimentally derived raw data, into equations used in his theoretical framework, because these data had been obtained from a variety of learning scenarios (p.223).

Addressing the fourth postulate, Hull (1943) believed in the fact that the central nervous system was not involved in behavior, because it was strictly a muscle/glandular response to stimuli (something similar, physiologically, to a "reflex-arc"). Hull explained this in detail with "certain coordinated movements are so universally required for survival and the conditions under which they occur are so uniform that automatic neural mechanisms are provided at birth for their execution" (p. 54). An example of this was an experiment that included the severing of a dog's spinal cord (above and forward of the hind legs) and the further stimulation of the bottom of one of the animal's hind feet. The foot would then curl its toes and attempt to "step" onto a hard surface and walk, even though there was no existing connection to the animal's spinal cord and obviously no connection to the central nervous system for this response (Hull, 1943).

A major addition to the field of behaviorism was that Hull (1943) was more intense about his treatment of peripheral responses to experimentally induced stimuli. Previous "behaviorists" (Thorndike, 1932; Guthrie, 1921) were somewhat vague about how some of these objective phenomena were explained. Hull was distinct about deductively describing certain types of objective behavioral responses peripherally, or as "spontaneous neural oscillations," that mediated a broad spectrum of observed responses (p. 310). This "peripheralism," concerning the previously mentioned intervening variables, was a major contribution to the field of behavioral psychology. Hull had descriptively set down his assessments of these contravening factors and had tied them to the mechanisms that arose from the objectively observed responses (Hull, 1943).

Watson (1924) put forward that the dual goals of behaviorist theory were to predict and control behavior. With observation, we can see that certain repeated behaviors can lead to generalizations about the raw data and that these can lead to the foundation of basic laws or postulates based upon science.

Opposing Schools of Behaviorist Thought: Skinner vs. Hull

Skinner and Hull both subscribed to Watson's four principal points that were the foundations of the theoretical framework of the theory of behaviorism. The means that these two behaviorists used to go about subscribing to those four points, however, differed with regard to each of their respective theoretical ideologies and their individual methods of application. Skinner's theory really was composed of two principal concepts: how and when the variables, intervening or otherwise, were applied in research into behavior; and certain events and how, since they were unobservable phenomena, those events were not really applicable for use as raw, empirical data in behavioral research.

The (Skinner, 1976) first area concerned the intervening variables that included "reflex reserve," "drive," and "emotion" (p. 245). These were grounded to the independent and dependent variables and different prospective operations, with regard to "operant conditioning," (p. 197) and were explained by how each of these related to one another. For example, keeping a test animal from receiving food could profoundly affect how the functions of *stimulus-response* "rates" and their reinforcement occurred, once the food was granted to the test subject (pp.249-250).

Skinner's (1976) second area was the notion of "Arminian Doctrine" (p. 60). These were the types of *stimulus-response* relationships that were not plainly evident to the naked eye, but they still transpired under the auspices of environmental, observable conditions. So, Skinner maintained that these doctrine events were coincidental by-products of the original variables that were actually, genuinely credited with the real cause of both hidden and observable behavior.

Skinner's events were synonymous with the type of hypothetical constructs espoused by Hull. So, Hull and Skinner were a part of the behaviorist theoretical school and used similar tools to advance behavioral theory. It is somewhat problematic that these types of theoretical constructs however were basically suppositions and not observable, raw, empirical data derived from experimental trials made upon subjects. Skinner did, however, reject "intersubjective agreement" (Hull, 1943) as a standard for observation in the sciences.

For Skinner (1976), if this standard rejection were to mean that an "operant response" (p.245), oral in nature, was considered to be the result of an "eliciting stimulus," (p. 244) then, in this respect, the stimulus would be considered to be an observation. So, by deduction, if doctrine events were not considered to be part of an hypothesis, or what is known in psychology as an "hypothetical construct" (Hull, 1943), then Skinner (1976) maintained that it would be observable phenomena and would become, in Skinnerian hypothesizing, part of the behavioral "data structure" (p. 93).

Skinner speaks of the doctrine events as suppositions. In some experiments, Skinner mentioned that the test subject observed these events, but the researcher who was actually conducting the study was said to have to suppose that the event had actually transpired. Second, there was no formalized proof that argued the point that these verbal responses, to environmental stimuli, actually obeyed the same postulates that the outwardly observable responses "observed." So, although Skinner acted as a verbal response editor for these inferred phenomena (Skinner, 1976), there was no solid evidence to support the notion that these events actually conformed to the tenets of the behavioral theoretical framework. In this extreme case, those events should have been considered as suppositions and were in actuality just hypothetical constructs, which dovetailed with the theorems of Hull's theoretical framework (Hull, 1943). Skinner and Hull had a number of ideological similarities.

With regard to the theoretical framework of behaviorism, Skinner disagreed with Hull's uses of "intervening variables and theoretical constructs" (Hull, 1943), so he seemed to deviate from the Hullian, behavioral platform. But, Skinner's own constructs seemed very similar to the Hullian ideology with regard to hypothetical constructs. After a review of a self-described summary of Skinner's (1976) experimental findings, one may note that he argued convincingly, but in the end was very similar, on theoretical grounds, to the theorizing of Hull. It was merely a matter of dimension and framework wherein small matters differed, but in the end, with regard to the major tenets of Hull's theoretical basis for behaviorism, Skinner followed Hull's framework for behaviorism with regard to theorizing, experimentation and the reporting of results (Skinner, 1976).

Although there were similarities to Hull's work, Skinner disliked intervening variables in general and hypothetical constructs in particular. This would also include Watson's (1924) physiological constructs and Hull's (1943) hypothetical (or strictly mental) constructs. Skinner disliked these two types of concepts because he felt that behaviorists should only concern themselves with observable behavior (Skinner, 1976) and since these were not observable, the behaviorist should not be concerned with these two concepts.

Skinner mentioned that at one time earlier in the history of research in general, these sorts of theorems (concepts) might have been appropriate, because adequate frameworks were lacking. But, since the intervening variables must be grounded in observable, raw data, these variables were supposed to be adequately descriptive of actual behavioral phenomena. In other words, there was only validity in research, with these previously described types of raw, empirical data, which was actually the result of observed behavior in test subjects. For this reason, in general, Skinner maintained that theory actually detracted from valid research in psychology (Skinner, 1976). Skinner rejected theory in general, because he stated that theorems were based upon untested postulates and since postulates were not originally, factually based, when the theory eventually goes out of fashion, all of the research that was associated with that theory was then of no consequence or intrinsic value.

Skinner showed, through his research, that his work could proceed without a large amount of theorizing and without "hypothetico-deductive" (Hull, 1943) theorems and postulates. First, Skinner objected to Hull's use of theorems and postulates and maintained that Hull was unsuccessful in his overall theoretical framework (Skinner, 1976). Hull admitted that his postulates were not necessarily able to be confirmed with raw, observable data from research, but that he was straight-forward about that point and was completely unconcerned (Hull, 1943).

Breadth Summary

This demonstration compared and contrasted Edward L. Thorndike's theory of connectionism with John B. Watson's theory of behaviorism and performed a critical analysis of how these two theorists directly contributed to the formation of the theory of behaviorism as it was later developed by its three principal developers: B.F. Skinner, Edwin R. Guthrie, and Clark L. Hull. This analysis was accomplished with an evaluation of the strengths and limitations of the tenets of behaviorist theory espoused through an evaluation of connectionism, the foundation of behaviorism and behaviorism's theoretical development by the three principal school's developers. The primary purpose of this analysis was to establish the framework for learning itself, how humans learn and of course to expound upon the foundation of the benchmarks for the establishment of the framework for the study of human personality.

There were three primary objectives for the accomplishment of this analysis. First, Edward L. Thorndike's theory of connectionism was analyzed as the foundation of *stimulus-response* psychology's theory of behaviorism with regard to the theory of connectionism's underlying principles and their eventual contribution to the formation of the theory of behaviorism. Second, although John B. Watson later attempted to refute connectionism, a foundational comparison and contrast of the two theories lead to a critical analysis of how these two theorists directly contributed to the formation of the theory of behaviorism, as it was later promulgated by the three principal developers of behaviorism. Third, an evaluation of the strengths and limitations of the tenets of behaviorist theory was provided, as espoused by behavioral theorists Skinner, Guthrie and Hull, for the purpose of relating how all five theorists' cumulative, theoretical work has contributed to how humans learn and to the establishment of some benchmarks concerning the framework for the study of human personality.

The techniques of theoretical comparison, one theorist with another's position or particular relation to the school of behaviorism, and the refinements of highlights from the various five theorists has been provided as a foundation for study in the next segment of this paper. Counseling will be explored in depth in the next segment, however, it is assumed that more critical study and research is needed into the analyses provided in the work of this segment, as more raw data become available from the continuing research in human psychology.

DEPTH
Annotated Bibliography

Amir, T., & Gati, I. (2006). Facets of career decision-making difficulties. *British Journal of Guidance & Counselling, 34*(4), 483-503. DOI: 10.1080/03069880600942608, 2008, from Academic Search Premier database.

This research was an exploration of the comparison and contrast between the test subjects' avowed versus their evaluated issues concerning their individual ability, as youthful adult applicants to a college or university, to make meaningful decisions concerning their prospective decisions about career choices. The results of the study demonstrated that the student test subjects, with regard to their evaluated versus demonstrated decisions about career choices, were mostly, positively correlated with the actual choices made. However, the evaluated versus the avowed stand-alone effectiveness of those choices, in some sectors of the research (relationships between scholastic aptitude and evaluated versus avowed career choice difficulties), were negatively correlated.

The research questions were well framed (five hypotheses were tested, from measured and expressed correlations that were high, through decidedness degree of choices) in that they were particular about the objectives and concise concerning the study's results. The significance, due to the high levels of positive correlation realized throughout the study, indicated that the results were mostly foreseen and significant. Intuitively, most researchers would assume, as these did (having given a survey of related, contemporary previous research in the article), that there would be a positive correlation overtone for the study in general. Concerning the way that the hypotheses for the study were posed and in how they were applied to the three general categories for study, the expected results were what was expected at the study's conclusion (the raw data received were broken down into ten research areas on the initial test subject questionnaire, and then further explored in the other five testing instruments).

The article made an original contribution to the existing body of knowledge in that it addressed the apparent dichotomy between the perceived difficulties and the actual difficulties in the students' ability to make effective career choices (and their actual effectiveness in eventually, actually making those career choices). However, this is only an expansion of previous like and type studies in this area (as indicated by citations by the researchers themselves, in their article). The theoretical framework for the study was appropriate in that it accurately addressed the difficulties, level of difficulties and the extent of those difficulties in the making of the career choices, with regard to perceived theory on the specific subject as well as the actual, evaluated results.

The researchers effectively communicated the results through discussions and mathematical representations of their results. The research method (299 students at an

Israeli university; 42% of the participants were female) was appropriate in that it took the actual opinions of hundreds of test subjects and then compared the opinions with actual results, communicating those comparisons through the framework (six actual test instruments from a background questionnaire through a psychometric test) of the research and the published article. There may be a better way to conduct this sort of research, but the method published in this particular article was more than adequate to support the results that were achieved by the researchers.

The sample size was adequate in that the sample included 299 youthful adults who participated as test subjects for the study published in the article. The actual sample, as reported by the researchers, may have biased the study in that the subjects were more mature than most subjects that could have been tested. Since they were Israeli students (there is an obligatory, national, military service requirement of 2-4 years), the sample was older than most prospective university applicants. The controls were set in that it was a broad enough sample to achieve results, but the study was not broken down in particular by gender, race or economic background (for example). This indicates that further research of these types of focused samples may be needed in order to generate results that are indicative of particular types of research subject groups. Since the sample was extremely general, without regard to some of the particular types of sampling that could have been conducted (with respect to gender, race or background), this may be indicative of a means to exclude their researcher bias (perceived or actual) and set into place a general framework (for future studies of this nature) that could then be specifically geared toward a more specific sampling.

The research should be replicable and the limitations of this study, as already discussed, were a lack of increased specificity with regard to more particular groups for study. The results are generalizable for a broad test subject group and the researchers indicated that other studies have achieved the same types of correlations. The conclusions are justified by the results, secondary to the test methods and hypotheses herein discussed above.

This article is valuable in that the research depicted supports previous findings from other, similar research studies and it can be useful in generalizing the results of this particular, broad type of study.

Betz, N., & Wolfe, J. (2005). Measuring confidence for basic domains of vocational activity in high school students. *Journal of Career Assessment, 13*(3), 251-270. DOI: 10.1177/1069072705274951, 2008, from Academic Search Premier database.

This study reported on an updated version of the Expanded Skills Inventory, which is conventionally used in counseling work with high school students, and expounded upon the evaluation and progress of this assessment instrument. The instrument is somewhat similar to the psychological study of the foundations area framework of the Strong Interest Inventory assessment tool. The newer version of the ESI exhibited results from a set of eight scales in 14 areas and it basically evaluated and reported a student's self-confidence with regard to interests in a variety of vocational areas.

Although the ESI was actually designed for use with high school students, this particular study used the instrument on 18 year old college freshmen. Since the students were evaluated in the fall quarter, they were still within several months of high school graduation. The research question was well framed and significant. This research was actually an outward growth of pre-existing current research on the topic and that research was effectively surveyed in the article. As an outgrowth, this research makes an original contribution to the existing body of knowledge.

The theoretical framework for the study was slightly adjusted for the test subjects to make the study more appropriate and some of the inapplicable areas were eliminated to refine the questions and improve the specificity of the results. The researchers communicated the results effectively through the use of mathematics and charts after applying the proper statistical evaluation methods. It appears that the researchers found a better way to perform the study and publish the results by adjusting the original assessment tool.

The sample size of 154 students, who were incoming freshman at a large college in the Midwest, was sufficient and there were adequate controls to help eliminate researcher bias. The research should be replicable with the original sample. The research should also be replicable with a proposed test subject pool of like and type subjects providing that the proposed test subject pool conforms to the applied constraints of demographics and vocational interests.

Although the results showed high positive correlations (most were above .50), the limitations of the study were

current assessment tool for use in this type of study. The sample size of 888 high school seniors was more than sufficient and the controls were very similar to the successful study upon which this study was originally based. The research is very replicable since the researchers have already replicated some of the original study. This is significant in that it forms a baseline for study, but it does not (unfortunately) give us the means for *further* study. There would be the means for *further* study if someone were to write a new evaluation tool or instrument.

This being said, there are some limitations to this study. It does not really break new psychological ground or have far-reaching consequences other than the fact that it drew to the fore the rationale that a new instrument was needed in order to engage in current, applicable, further study. The findings are generalizable and the conclusions, just like in the previous study, were certainly justified by the results.

Blustein, D., Kenna, A., Gill, N., & Devoy, J. (2008). The psychology of working: A new framework for counseling practice and public policy. *The Career Development Quarterly, 56*(4), 294-308. Document ID: 1502846901, 2008, from ProQuest Central database.

The authors of this study featured a different avenue of examination from the more traditional self-efficacy model wherein the test subjects had the free will and the means to make those selections. This particular venue was the worker mode and the subjects did not have the more selective subjects' abilities accorded to the individuals involved in other studies. The authors changed the actual framework, as opposed to that normally accepted as conventional in other studies, by looking at the test subjects from the worker viewpoint. The authors contended that this was more of a fair and legitimate viewpoint that has applicability to real world situations. In this manner, the authors contended that there was a more appropriate framework for career counselors to apply their skills and help students make better, more appropriate vocational choices.

With regard to the survey of current literature and applicable studies, the survey evaluated current and pre-existing studies. These studies were discussed from the viewpoints of the psychology of work and how humans view work itself, such as the components of survival, social interfacing and self-expression. There was a summary of some of the issues that could affect a practice in counseling.

There actually was a research question, but there were no test subjects (there were, if one were to include the subjects used in the studies quoted in this article). The research was the existing body of knowledge. In other words, the researchers quoted all of the existing research and merely changed the framework. The study made a contribution to the existing body of knowledge by framing a new framework for future researchers who choose to do research along these lines, but approach that new research from this redefined, different perspective.

This article was not necessarily a study, but a conceptual paper that discussed a different framework for use in future studies. Therefore, most of the standard annotation questions didn't really apply to this article.

There really was no study involving new test subjects, so the theoretical framework was just rhetoric. The researchers communicated everyone else's work, to bolster their own statements, but they did not discover anything that could be described as 'new.' This was a discussion promoting a different viewpoint for prospective research, so there really was not a particular research method. It was appropriate in that the researchers used other scholars' work to support their thesis. Therefore, the questions regarding a better way *to research* was proposed, but there was no sample size, controls or a question of being replicable.

The limitations to the study were that all of the existing research was used to bolster the researchers' statements about how a change in the viewpoint and framework for studies in general could change. The findings were pretty general, but they are probably not generalizable in the sense that there were no test subjects or raw data in this study. It was just a re-statement of previous research with a different twist of perspective and viewpoints for potential, future study. The conclusions that a more adequate framework for future study is needed are probably just. Many studies use test subjects who exhibit self-efficacy and privilege and this study concluded that it would probably be more current and applicable to use test subjects from the working class to make future studies more contemporary and applicable for counseling uses.

Duffy, R., & Sedlacek, W. (2007). The work values of first-year college students: Exploring group differences. *The Career Development Quarterly, 55*(4), 359-364. Document ID: 1297141131, 2008, from ProQuest Central database.

The article was the publication of research concerning the analysis of surveys of first year college students. The students selected for this research were concerned about long-term issues that affected their careers. Ten work values were assessed in the survey, to give the researchers data for their analyses, and then these data were sub-divided into four groups. The researchers claimed that more reliable means could have been used, if more space and time had been available. As it was, 93% of all incoming freshmen were assessed for the study at a particular college and it was performed through a single line item in about thirty minutes' worth of a survey given to that group.

The resulting research was properly framed later in the study and was significant because there were demographic considerations concerning these data. The study was broken down by group distinctions, such as aspirations, family income and the work issues themselves. Race and gender also figured prominently in the assessment of these data. The research was properly related to the current body of knowledge by showing where the research continued, beyond the results of previous studies cited. Thus, the article made an original contribution to the existing body of knowledge by continuing pre-existing research and it provided a more select, limited framework to study in

and the will to even endure vocational counseling, but also the perception of the eventual outcomes concerning expectations. The research related well to the existing body of knowledge in that it did an adequate job in the survey of previous studies and an even more effective placement, of the study itself, as a continuation of that previous research in the accomplishment of an original contribution.

The theoretical framework was adequate and appropriate and the researchers communicated their findings and the extrapolated results clearly and fully. The research method was appropriate in that it used quantitative means and statistically answered the research questions with plainly reported results. There might have been a better way to find the answers to the research questions. However, it would have involved a tremendously larger sample size and would not have been convincingly worth the increased time and effort, since the new results would not have been statistically more meaningful. The reason for this was that the sample size was sufficient, there were adequate controls and the research was eminently replicable.

This being said, the statements made were really a function of the limitations of the study. For example, to make generalized statements about gender concerning these research questions, it would have been a more certain result with a larger sample size. But, from the scientific and statistical viewpoints, the statements made could be drawn from the adequate sample size depicted in the framework and results that were secondary to this study. The findings are generalizable and the conclusions are justified by the results, from statistical and scientific viewpoints.

Ganske, K., & Ashby, J. (2007). Perfectionism and career decision-making self-efficacy. *Journal of Employment Counseling, 44*(1), 17-28. Document ID: 1230709241, 2008, from ABI/INFORM Global database.

Ganske & Ashby (2007) provided an examination of certain linkages between "perfectionism and career decision-making self-efficacy." The test subjects engaged in the study participated in an abbreviated assessment tool and it was determined by the researchers that the subjects who were "adaptive" were more prone to a more advanced level of individual self-reliance in the subjects' own abilities to make vocational or career choices as opposed to those subjects who were "maladaptive." There was a segment of subjects in the study who were identified as "maladaptive perfectionists and nonperfectionists" and these two groups, as a finding of this study, did not experience a marked increase in their respective abilities to make self-reliant, individual decisions about vocational choices or career choices in general (p.17).

The research questions were well framed and significant in that they extended the current research into the study. The existing, contemporary research was extensively surveyed by the researchers and the research related well to the existing body of knowledge. The article, as published findings of the study, made an original contribution to the existing body of knowledge. It published results about the fact that it contributed to the current pool of knowledge that suggests that, with regard to vocational and career choices made by the subject test pool, perfectionism has ingredients of both the aforementioned adaptive and maladaptive behaviors.

The theoretical framework for the study was adequate and appropriate and the researchers communicated clearly and fully their results along with the results' implications, with regard to contemporary vocational counseling and the implications for further study in this area. The research method was appropriate and although there may be a better way to find answers to the research questions, the researchers did an adequate job of handling the research questions.

The sample size of 201 college students was sufficient and there were adequate controls to account for researcher bias. However, the subject sample was skewed by gender and race toward the female gender in that almost 82% of the test subjects were female and the race participant breakdown was slanted toward the caucasian subject pool with a representation of 92%. Obviously, these were not demonstrative of the general pool of most universities that could have been chosen for this study; midwestern or otherwise. The research is replicable, but the results might differ slightly with a different mix of gender and race in an alternate test pool of subjects taken from perhaps a university in another area of the country.

The limitations of the study were that it was specific about what it was going to use for hypotheses to be tested against the raw data from a 23 item survey of 201 test subjects comprised of college students who were about 23 years of age. However, it may not be representative enough to be generalizable, because of the skewed representations of gender and race in the test pool of subjects who were surveyed. However, the conclusions, in the isolated framework of how the hypotheses were framed and related to the current research, were justified by the results of the study.

Harrington, T., & Harrington, J. (2007). Every one has abilities, but do counselors know how to assess all abilities and use this information? *Career Planning & Adult Development Journal,* *23*(2), 22-29. Document ID: 1357499631, 2008, from ProQuest Central database

This study poses the rhetorical question concerning whether or not counselors know what to do with students who demonstrate varied abilities and interests. The article discussed the interpretation of the results of an assessment tool (Ability Explorer) so that counselors could more appropriately work with students concerning the matching of intrinsic abilities to educational opportunities, as well as to career goals. The foundation for the use of the assessment instrument, and its interpretation, was that the researchers felt that society will be in a better position if individuals were allowed the opportunity to use all of their intrinsic abilities and hidden talents. In this way, the researchers felt that the individual would be happier and more productive.

The research question was well framed and was significant, since it enlarged upon the present, but more appropriate usage of a pre-existing assessment instrument. It was well related to the existing body of knowledge because it took existing research in counseling and psychology, and it enlarged upon what was already in use. So, it made an original contribution to the existing body of knowledge by expounding upon a more appropriate and effective use of a currently used assessment instrument.

The researchers communicated, through the use of steps, their work as it evolved through the use of the assessment instrument. The basis was echoed in the conclusion: that the U.S. Census reported that almost two-thirds of incoming, college freshmen did not take into account their basic abilities with regard to educational and career choices.

Larson, L., & Borgen, F. (2006). Do personality traits contribute to vocational self-efficacy? *Journal of Career Assessment, 14*(3), 295-311. DOI: 10.1177/1069072706286446, 2008, from SAGE Journals Online.

Larson and Borgen (2006) cite research that indicated that personality was perceived to preclude "self-efficacy and interest development," but they went on to say that there was not a wealth of research that indicated that there was an actual link between "personality and self-efficacy." Their research actually acted as a link between personality and self-efficacy through the introduction of results from four universities. The researchers related the use of several assessment instruments and measured the purported links between personality and self-efficacy within a framework of 11 individualized areas of personality and a summary group of three more general areas. In this way, the researchers were able to show positive correlations and some links to the increase in career confidence interests and tendencies among the test subject students (p. 295).

The research questions were well-framed in that they were specifically designed to bridge the gap between the study's extensive literature survey, which confirmed that there was insufficient evidence currently present to perform the linkages questioned by the researchers, and the hypotheses of the researchers' study. Thus, the research questions were significant in that they attempted to promote an extended search beyond the current body of research to bring new information into the foreground. The research was directly related to the existing body of knowledge in that it was an extension of what was presently held as a working theory. Further, this study made an original contribution to the existing body of knowledge by completing the train of evidence that supported the linkages between personality and self-efficacy.

The theoretical framework for the study was adequate and appropriate and the researchers communicated clearly and fully the regimen, correlations and results after a thorough literature survey. The research method was appropriate and there may have been a better way to find the answers to the research questions, but the researchers were thorough and effective in their methodologies. The sample sizes at the four midwestern universities were taken over a period of various semesters spanning 2-years and each sample consisted of over 250 students (two samples were 300 plus). The controls were sufficient to allow for researcher bias and the research, based upon stratified time length, methods and sample size, should be replicable.

The limitations of the study were very specific in order to obtain specific results for the linkages delineated herein above. Thus, since the questions and results were specific, regarding large enough sample sizes and the resulting consistency of findings obtained and communicated, the findings should be generalizable. There was enough of a pre-existing platform, in the literature survey of previous studies that established a clear link to this study (along with the rigorous methodologies employed in this study), to warrant that the conclusions are justified by the results.

Miller, M. (2007). Examining the degree of congruency between a traditional career instrument and an online self-assessment exercise. *Journal of Employment Counseling, 44*(1), 11-16. Document ID: 1230709231, 2008, from ABI/INFORM Global database.

Miller (2007) evaluated and compared the findings of a traditional assessment tool, with respect to "career planning," to the results derived from an "online self-assessment career planning exercise" in order to determine the relationships between the two and whether or not there were similarities. The results of the study claimed that there were similarities between these assessment tools and that there were certain indications for counselors, who performed advising in vocational and career areas. There were also some suggestions for areas of further study, which arose secondary to this study and the publication of the results in this article.

The research questions were well framed and significant in that they enlarged upon the existing body of knowledge, exhibited in the extensive survey in this article. The article made an original contribution to the existing body of knowledge in that it extended knowledge of the current base as a result of the publication of the findings in this study. The theoretical framework of the study was adequate and appropriate and the researcher communicated the results clearly and fully. Even though the research method was appropriate, there may have been a better way to find answers to the research questions.

There were some issues with the diversity of the pool of test subjects involved in the study. This pool of test subjects was different from that of the other studies annotated herein above, in that there were some diversity issues involved. For example, instead of hundreds of test subjects in the test subject pool, there were only 35 subjects. Although other studies depicted herein above researched a pool of test subjects who were nearly graduated high school students, high school graduates in transition or beginning undergraduate students, this study only used graduate students. There were also some stratified sample diversity issues regarding the breakdown of test subjects with relation to race and gender: women outweighed men by more than a margin of 2:1; Afro-Americans in the study approached a composition of almost 30% of the subject test pool; and some of the subjects were almost 60 years of age. Thus, the sample size was insufficient, the diversity and group breakdowns of the sample of test subjects were skewed and the subjects, with regard to age, were far more mature than the test pool composition of most of the other studies annotated herein.

The considerations that made this study important

business direction for the students to eventually pursue, with regard to the test subjects' studies in the college's business curriculum.

The research well related to the existing body of knowledge and expanded upon the brief literature survey published in the article. The article made an original contribution to the existing body of knowledge by expanding upon the survey and filling a gap in the existing knowledge with regard to a more practical application of the original BOSS program to more contemporary students in the studied, subject test pool. The theoretical framework for the study was adequate and appropriate in that it narrowly defined the questions to be researched and then followed through with an eventual demonstration of the applicability and positive correlations demonstrated by the results and a discussion secondary to the statistical results achieved with the data harvested in the study.

The researchers communicated clearly and fully the results of the study and included a variety of theoretical questions prompting the reader to think about ways in which a further study could be conducted to validate (or corroborate) the present study and break new ground in an attempt to refine certain points addressed in the study, that were not fully researched due to the limited nature and principal foci of this particular study. The research methods were appropriate and they were narrowly defined enough in order to sufficiently (and efficiently) conduct this study. There may have been a better way to find the answers through the use of a larger study sample; the test pool of subjects was comprised of 35 incoming freshmen from across the state of Mississippi.

There were adequate controls present to account for

researcher bias and the research was done in such a way that it should be replicable. One of the limitations of the study was the small sample size. Thus, if the research were duplicated and it was hoped that the results of this study were replicable, due to a higher incidence of statistical certainty, the results of a further study with a larger sample might be slightly more accurate due to the results of a larger test pool of subjects surveyed.

The findings of this study are generalizable for a stratified sampling of southern, economically disadvantaged students, but some researchers might wish to see a larger subject test pool and these other researchers would probably realize that this study would not be generalizable to the general population of all incoming college freshmen. However, some conclusions could be drawn if the results of this study were practically applied to the incoming freshman population of a technical college where business subjects are taught. Based upon the narrow confines of the parameters for this study, the conclusions are justified by the results.

Nauta, M. (2007). Career interests, self-efficacy, and personality as antecedents of career exploration. *Journal of Career Assessment, 15*(2), 162-180. DOI: 10.1177/1069072706298018, 2008, from SAGE Journals Online.

The author conducted a prediction study of the career actualization results of a test of college students (1 1/2 years into the future) based upon the use of Holland's assessment instrument and the basic areas of personality. She used controls for the actual current year of educational attainment and gender in order to be more results specific in the study with regard to forecasted career decisions made by the students comprising the test pool of the study. She reached a variety of conclusions from the study's results, with regard to some personality and assessed traits, associated with anticipated results.

The research question was well framed and significant in that, with regard to the literature survey performed within the publication of the study, there had not previously been a significant attempt to take an assessment tool, dove-tailed with personality, to perform this sort of forecasting stemming from a test pool of subjects. The research related well to the existing body of knowledge, and extended that research to make an original contribution to the existing body of knowledge.

The theoretical framework for the study was adequate and appropriate and the researcher communicated the results clearly and fully. The research method was appropriate for the nature of the study, since it followed-up a previous study that had extended those results in order to provide answers for the career forecast. The research method was appropriate, but in the follow-up, the test subject sample was somewhat skewed. The original subject study (18 months earlier) was comprised of 251 subjects who were college students. The student test pool was relatively well distributed between race, gender and other groupings. However, this study follow-up with those subjects and, based upon test subjects who could not be reached, resulted in a test pool for follow-up comprised of only 113 students. The grouping, for example, was composed of 10% Afro-American and 86% Caucasian test subjects. Unfortunately, 89% of the new subjects in the test pool were female. This makes a somewhat altered sample and affected the generalizability of the study's results, with regard to gender. There might have been a better way to find answers to the research questions, and it would certainly have involved a more representative sample of test subjects in the pool with regard to a breakdown by gender.

The sample size was sufficient for narrow conclusions to be drawn and there were adequate controls for researcher bias. The research, with this gender-skewed, non-representative sample of college students, would probably be replicable. The limitations of the study were that less than half of the original subjects studied actually survived, for test purposes, to be included in the current study's test pool of subjects. This precluded generalizability of the study's findings, in conjunction with the current gender-skewed test pool studied. However, for the manner in which the hypotheses were worded, the conclusions are justified by the results.

Patton, W., & Creed, P. (2007). Occupational aspirations and expectations of Australian adolescents. *Australian Journal of Career Development, 16*(1), 46-59. Document ID: 1393446261, 2008, from ABI/INFORM Global database.

The authors used the basic six categories in the Holland model, as an assessment instrument for the accumulation of raw data, and compared the differences between proposed career decisions and the desired choices of high school student test subjects. The various associations, between varieties of sub-topics, provided the interplay for the hypotheses in the study and worked well within that framework in order to provide a solid direction for the research platform and the study's eventual results. The study validated the intuitive observations that the student subjects, who were not well-versed in career information and who were not strong scholastically, tended to choose a career in the vocational or semi-skilled trades. Further, the students who were more well-informed and stronger scholastically, tended to choose a professional career.

The research questions were well-framed and significant. Although this study may seem to be repetitive of some of the other research surveyed, the literature survey indicated that this study was necessary and filled a void. The research was related to the existing body of knowledge in that it extended contemporary research by conducting this study to answer the hypotheses posed, which heretofore had not been completely answered by other researchers in their published studies. Therefore, the study made an original contribution to the existing body of knowledge by extending the previous research platform to include the sub-topics secondary to Holland's assessment instrument, with an application to perceived versus actual career aspirations and expectations of adolescents (grades 8-12).

The theoretical framework for the study was adequate and appropriate and the researchers communicated clearly and fully the results of the study. The research methods were appropriate and there did not seem to be a better way to find answers to the research questions posed in this study. The sample size of 333 test subjects, who were adolescents at an Australian suburban school, averaged 15 years of age and was divided approximately evenly by gender. The sample size was sufficient and there were adequate controls in place to account for researcher bias. The research results, if given a sample that duplicated the test subject pool, should be replicable.

Although the study was conducted using adolescents in Australia, this should not necessarily preclude the study's results, due to any inherent limitations, from being generalizable with regard to the study's findings. The conclusions, which were intuitive before the study was made, are justified by the results.

Tang, M., Pan, W., & Newmeyer, M. (2008). Factors influencing high school students' career aspirations. *Professional School Counseling, 11*(5), 285-295. Document ID: 1490316191, 2008, from ProQuest Central database.

Tang et al. (2008) analyzed the issues that affect students with regard to the students' concerns about a career. The authors utilized an instrument that used, as its interactive framework, the individual's independence concerning decisions and their hopes regarding eventual career selection. The independence and hopes views were synthesized with "career interests and career choices," in order to correlate the eventual process results with respect to high school students of different genders (p. 285).

The research question was well framed and significant. This study used an assessment instrument to compile data with regard to how a number of different aspects of the self-independence of career choice could interact with other considerations, as applied to the choices pursued by the high school student test subjects of different genders. The research, as depicted by the extensive survey of existing studies, was well related to the existing body of knowledge. It made an original contribution in that it extended the current research from the previous research as a framework, and sought to provide study results that brought fresh insight to the field.

The theoretical framework for the study was adequate and appropriate and the researchers communicated the results clearly and fully. The research method was somewhat skewed toward females in that the percentage of test subjects was 81 females to 60 males; they were all students at a high school in the suburbs of the Midwest. The public school students averaged about 16 years of age and this age was appropriate for career counseling, with regard to the usual timeframe for the counseling of high school students concerning the students' prospective desire to attend college or a vocational school after high school graduation.

Although the research method was appropriate, there were better ways to find answers to the research questions (there were three questions posed as hypotheses). If the test subject sample pool were larger than N=141 and if a breakdown, by gender, of student subjects was closer to the actual population's percentage (in the general population after graduation, to make the results "more" generalizable), then there may be a more refined set of correlated results that could have been attained. However, the sample size was sufficient and there were adequate controls to account for researcher bias. If the researchers were to choose a similar breakdown of high school students from the suburbs of the Midwest, taken from a public school system, then the results would have been more than likely to have been replicable.

The limitations of the study were that the test subjects did not adequately represent the traditional societal percentages that one would expect in the general population. By percentage of race, concerning the test subjects in the study, nearly 92% of the test subjects in the survey pool were caucasian. Thus, the other races were not proportionally represented, as they would traditionally be in the general population nationwide (for example). This limitation, along with the previously discussed gender test subject breakdowns, could conceivably affect the generalizable nature of the study's findings. However, the conclusions are justified by the results. There were enough statistical, positive correlations, with regard to the questions posed in the original three hypotheses, to make the study results valid.

Wolniak, G., & Pascarella, E. (2007). Initial evidence on the long-term impacts of work colleges. *Research in Higher Education, 48*(1), 39-71. DOI: 10.1007/ s11162-006-9023-6, 2008, from Academic Search Premier database.

Wolniak and Pascarella (2007) performed a study, on the eventual results with regard to work and academics, of the difference between students who attended a college that emphasized career work versus attendance at more traditional private colleges and public universities. The questions sought to augment pre-existing literature with an exploration of students who were in-transition between high school and college, with regard to work and their resulting collegiate results. Also, the authors sought to explore some colleges that have been outside the purview of more conventional research. The research questions were well framed and significant in that they were an extension of the existing body of knowledge. A brief survey of the existing literature was made by the authors and this article made an original contribution to the existing body of knowledge because it expanded upon the dearth of previously published research on the topic.

The Wolniak and Pascarella (2007) theoretical framework attempted to respond to three questions in the conduct of the research: what are the individual results of attendance at a "work college," as opposed to traditional institutions; how do the individual effects of work colleges differ, with regard to "employment" and "rewards," compared with the traditional schools; and are the individual effects specific or can they be generalized and are the individual effects the same for all students or just for some with "different characteristics" (p. 42)?

The researchers communicated clearly and fully and the research method, utilizing the quantitative method, was appropriate. There may be a better way to find answers to the research question, but it would involve an extremely large sample size and would differ only negligibly from the results already presented in this study. The sample size was sufficient and involved over 7,000 graduates from 30 colleges over the period of 25 years. There were adequate controls to account for researcher bias and the research is replicable, based upon the statistical results presented in the study's conclusions.

The limitations of the study were that the questions

asked were very specific and were answered specifically by the statistical correlations and the summary of research results. In other words, the specificity of the questions and the answers to those questions made the results more generalizable, because of the large sample, research methods and the manner in which the conclusions were presented. The conclusions are justified by the results, and this research provides a solid platform for further study of these data, the stated, answered questions and new research that evolves from additional data accumulated over time.

Literature Review Essay

Career Interests and vocational confidence

Nauta (2007) maintained that career interests and vocational confidence were not mutually exclusive. Larson and Borgen (2006) more conclusively expanded upon this view and did find positive correlations between "personality and confidence correlations" in their 1,173 student sample, as it related to two integral factors: achievement and social potency. Larson and Borgen explicitly stated that, "two of PEM's primary scales (Social Potency and Achievement) were consistently related to the mean confidence level" (p. 303). This research demonstrated a conclusive link between *career interests and vocational confidence.*

Amir and Gati (2006) found that there were some important correlations between factors that influenced the degree of vocational confidence. These researchers conclusively found that "the correlations between measured and expressed difficulties were high in all three major categories: 0.84 for the lack of readiness, 0.89 for lack of information, and 0.74 for inconsistent information" (pp. 492-493). These differences measured the effects of vocational confidence in the student population studied. As a result of the high, positive correlations demonstrated in their study, there was a profound difference between the two aspects of what a student perceived to be the career making difficulty and what the student actually accomplished with regard to career decision making.

Bloxom et al (2008) noted that approximately 80% of students who were about to graduate from high school felt that it was important "to pursue a career that requires post-secondary education or training" (p.87). Moore et al., (2007) was a study that demonstrated the positive results concerning a multiple year program that promoted and developed incoming college students who hailed from sub-economic backgrounds. The program, entitled "BOSS Camp (Business Opportunities for Success School)," was designed to integrate the economically underprivileged students into a conventional business program at an undergraduate college. The program served to function as a "bridging" mechanism to indoctrinate the incoming students (during the pre-summer break) with the success requirements of that program. The researchers contended that this interim bridging mechanism inculcated the incoming disadvantaged students with the necessary attributes that eventually contributed to the students' eventual success in the college's business program (p. 1). The entire rationale for the BOSS program in particular, was to stimulate career interest among the incoming population of disadvantaged students, who planned to attend an undergraduate business college. As a function of that stimulated interest, the program was designed to work on the practical aspects of vocational confidence through a series of assessment instruments and sub-programs that taught learning by "doing" to the students.

Betz and Wolfe (2005) determined, based upon the two studies that the researchers performed, that the new 8-item scale (added to their surveyed Holland themes) proved to be a more accurate predictor of vocational confidence and career interests, than just the traditional assessment instrument previously used in other studies (that were surveyed earlier in the publication of the results of their study). There were some ethnic and race issues that the researchers had not expected. For example, in a school system where only about one-third of the students (overall) expected to attend college, there was an extremely high vocational confidence level among the African-American student population; over 85% of the African-American student population intended to attend college after high school graduation. Therefore, the researchers determined that "this represents a vast difference between intentions and probable actual behavior" (p. 268).

The results achieved in study 2 (of the two studies discussed), with the added 8-item scale, were unexpected results and those results were not expected in the original hypotheses generated as the premises for this study. Betz and Wolfe (2005) mentioned that further study was needed in the area of ethnic and race variables, with regard to career interests and vocational confidence, in this type of student sample. The researchers indicated that a better instrument was needed, so this suggested the need for a theoretical construct of a counseling instrument that would direct these students in the absence, or with minimal input from, counseling professionals with regard to career counseling and a career choice.

Patton and Creed (2007) found in their study results that there were strong career interests in their student subject pool because "students generally aspired to and expected to work within four occupational categories (investigative, social, artistic and realistic), and especially rejected conventional and enterprising occupations as aspirations and expectations" (p. 55). The researchers found an extremely strong positive correlation among the variables used to predict this sort of occupational behavior, associated with expectations involving career interests. However, there were some issues involved with findings regarding vocational confidence that arose from their study. The researchers found that "analyses identified that students who held different RIASEC aspirations to expectations were more career indecisive, held expectations for lower status jobs, had lower self-esteem, lower career goals and poorer career development attitude[s] than their non-discrepant peers" (p. 56). With regard to the higher positive correlations involved with the study's results (concerning career interests), the results were not as strong concerning vocational confidence and the researchers were compelled to side with findings from the literature survey that indicated that more research, into the area of vocational confidence, was needed.

Ganske and Ashby (2007) determined, in the results of their study, that "in this study, we found that adaptive perfectionists had greater career decision-making self-efficacy when compared with maladaptive perfectionists." Since this was one of the tests that related the attributes of *career interests and vocational confidence*, this study showed a relationship between the two. The researchers determined that one of the possible reasons for this relationship was the "self-appraisal" component of adaptive perfectionists and how that group tended to view themselves, with relation to career interests and the impact of those interests. When those interests manifested in the decision-making process, and their related strength was utilized (perceived as vocational confidence), the resulting career counseling process changed and better choices were evidently made by the subject test pool participants (p. 24).

Blustein, Kenna, Gill, and Devoy (2008) determined that those from disadvantaged backgrounds did not have a "strong voice" when it came to the concepts of career interests and vocational confidence. The researchers specifically stated that these were the students who did not have access to formalized counseling and that these were not the types of students that professionals addressed in professional discussions (p. 304). This invited the use of a yet to be written school-to-work assessment tool that would specifically address the counseling needs of students in a work-based education. This is a concern that will be addressed in the Application segment of this paper - a theoretical construct of a counseling instrument that will direct these students in the absence, or with minimal input from, counseling professionals with regard to career counseling and a career choice.

Fouad, Chen, Guillen, Henry, Kantemneni, Novacovic, Priester, and Terry (2007) determined, based upon the results of an assessment instrument administered to their study's 159 college student sample, that there was a significant amount of career interest concerns among the test subject population. In fact, the researchers found that, in their test subject sample, "out of the 453 concerns included, 239 were categorized as career concerns." With regard to the "Vocational Expectations Questionnaire," the students indicated that they were not comfortable (with relation to the control group), with their level of vocational confidence and felt that the career counseling that they did receive should have done more than just advise them concerning career choices. Some even felt that the career counseling session should have decided for the student what course to follow for a career, completely absolving the student of any responsibility with, or for, the decision-making process (p. 24). The results of this study, as portrayed by the interpretation given by the researchers, indicated that students were not content with the specific counseling received during the career counseling process. This suggested the need for a theoretical construct of a counseling instrument that would direct these students in the absence, or with minimal input from, counseling professionals with regard to career counseling and a career choice.

Duffy and Sedlacek (2007) determined that the test subjects in their research sample were divided along specific lines, when the aspects of career interests and vocational confidence were considered. The researchers found that the students who were interested in professional, graduate degrees were more interested in "prestige," and those who sought only an undergraduate degree were interested in "intrinsic values" such as social responsibility. The sample results determined that the vocational confidence was aligned along the lines wherein those who were from family income backgrounds of "$75,000-$124,999," were prone to choose values such as social responsibility, whereas those students who were from disadvantaged or wealthy backgrounds exhibited the vocational confidence to choose "extrinsic values," such as high income (p. 361).

Self-efficacy and personality

Nauta (2007) concluded that only a single self-efficacy type (artistic) was specifically shown to be exclusive to self-efficacy regarding career choice, and that this variable was also specifically tied to gender. She further concluded that there were exhibited traits that were conclusively a function of self-efficacy, and that there were certain relationships with those exhibited traits: being extraverted was a trait that was negatively correlated and "openness" was a trait that was positively correlated. Nauta did conclude that, "when interests, self-efficacy, and personality variables were added in the second steps, they did not account for a significant change in the proportion of environmental exploration scores explained" (p. 172). Therefore, she literally explained, with empirical evidence, that these factors associated with self-efficacy and personality, were not a part of the search behavior of these students once they started to examine prospective environments for work.

Larson and Borgen (2006) specifically stated, with regard to personality, that their results demonstrated that there were "overlaps with vocational interests and vocational confidence with similar and unique linkages" (p. 306). To enlarge upon this, and make a specific stand with regard to the content of their study, Larson and Borgen concluded with, "our results also show that personality matters tremendously in many aspects of career self-efficacy" (p.307). These studies showed a link, positively correlated as a result of the results from the studies, that there was a positive linkage between self-efficacy and personality.

Harrington and Harrington (2007) stated in their study that, "counselors need to be sensitive to possible interpretation regarding an individual's self-efficacy beliefs." The researchers continued with the rationale that counselors sometimes failed to make the link between *self-efficacy and personality,* because the assessment instrument results didn't indicate an actual interest or talent to support the counseling client's perceived interest in a career (p. 27). The researchers continued with the results that career counselors may not be as successful as the reports have indicated, since the U.S. Census Bureau reported that 2 out of 3 high school graduates were uncertain about their own innate abilities, or even which major or interest to pursue in college (p. 28).

Amir and Gati (2006) found that there was a strong correlation between self-efficacy and the personality elements involved in career decision-making skills. Their primary finding had specifically to do with "the cognitive aspects of vocational decision-making styles" (p. 497). Therefore, the students' comprehension and overall understanding of the process, along with the use of their personality elements, had a significant impact upon their career, decision-making self-efficacy.

Tang, Pan, and Newmeyer (2008) conducted a study that explored the relationships between various personality factors, and the resulting relationships between those factors that developed into the making of career choices. One of the variables that the researchers explored in their study was self-efficacy, as a personality factor that affected career decision aspirations and choices. In this particular study, "***career*** self-efficacy was defined operationally in this study as individuals' perception of their competence in ***career*** activities" (p. 6). The results of the study indicated that the factor that was strongest, with the relationship between *personality and self-efficacy,* was the expected outcome. Of the eight prospective outcomes studied, there was a high, positive correlation related directly to the clients' expected outcomes. It was demonstrated that expectations could play a large role, when it came to the eventual decision-making process, in the relationship between personality and eventual, career, decision-making self-efficacy.

Betz and Wolfe (2005) indicated that their new 8-item supplement, to the pre-existing assessment instruments, actually lowered the achieved results of the correlations regarding self-efficacy and personality. However, the traditional, gender-based results, found in the previous studies which the researchers had surveyed in their study's published results, were consistent with results achieved in the two new studies. Males correspondingly did better in the mechanical aspects of career-based personality attributes, whereas females performed better in the "Helping and Cultural Sensitivity" personality attributes (p. 265). With the traditional attributes considered, the new 8-item index actually lowered the correlations that the researchers hoped to achieve and they contended that further study, with regard to assessment instruments, was needed.

Patton and Creed (2007) moved away from the

literature survey in their research and characterized the relationship between self-efficacy and personality in a new manner, when they explicitly stated that the researcher "recognises [sic] the relevance of the self-efficacy construct or self-concept, represented in the current study as self-esteem." Based upon the correlations achieved in their study, the researchers believed that by accumulating data from the subject pool in this manner, that the data lent themselves to be more effective "transition points" and were more effective in the eventual results analysis (p.56). The re-characterization worked, because the researchers had strong, positive data correlation among the variables, when these traits were collected and interpreted as self-esteem.

Ganske and Ashby (2007) stated in their study that "the purpose of this study was to evaluate the relationship between multidimensional perfectionism and career decision-making self-efficacy" (p. 23). The researchers conclusively showed that there was a direct relationship between these two variables, as the direct result of a high, statistical, positive correlation. The researchers even stated that it was the career counselor's obligation to improve the client's self-efficacy, in order to facilitate appropriate responses to counseling in order to use personality attributes to make eventual, career decisions (p. 20).

Prediction of career search behavior

Nauta (2007) determined, based upon three sets of regression analyses of the data in her study, that *self* and other certain factors, such as exploration of the student's *environment,* were not related. Therefore, she did further investigations to determine what other issues or factors may have been extant, for the relationships involved that fostered behavior that encouraged career search. In her first analysis, she did determine that *year in school* and *gender* were adequate predictors, with regard to career search behavior (p. 172).

Larson and Borgen (2006) stated in their study that, "empirical results in this article and those we have cited show that personality matters in career behavior. Personality matters in career interests and self-efficacy, career development, career choice, job performance, and job satisfaction" (p. 308). More specifically, this clearly meant that the prediction of career search behavior was predicated upon personality and that personality was a benchmark (Thorndike, 1932). Thus, Larson and Borgen (2006) explained that this set into place a framework for the remainder of the extant behaviors, which characterized the career search in particular: career interests and self-efficacy, career development, career choice, job performance, and job satisfaction (p. 308).

Amir and Gati (2006) reported that "those who reported higher degrees of decidedness had fewer difficulties in career decision-making, reported higher career decision-making self-efficacy, and could be characterised [sic] by a thinking (rather than feeling) decision-making style" (p. 498). Thus, the prediction of career search behavior was skewed by the level of decidedness in the actual population of students studied in the research sample of this study. A further conclusion of the study was that those students who were more advanced in their respective programs of study, had less difficulty with career decision-making. The students' eventual employment would be predicated upon their immediate skill employed in the job search, for a position after graduation.

Tang, Pan, and Newmeyer (2008) conducted a study that explored the relationships between various personality factors and the resulting relationships between those factors that developed into the making of career choices. One of the variables that the researchers explored in their study was outcome expectation, as a personality factor that affected career decision aspirations and choices. The results of the study indicated that a factor, with relationship between personality and the *prediction of career search behavior,* was the expected outcome. Of the eight prospective outcomes studied, there was a particularly high positive correlation related directly to the clients' expected outcomes. It was demonstrated that expectations played a large role when it came to the eventual decision-making process in the relationship between personality, and prediction of career search behavior.

Bloxom et al (2008) found that there were items in a framework, seven in all, that contributed to the prediction of career search behavior. The main, most highly correlated examples, of these types of search behaviors, were different types of personal interests and links between those interests and the career itself. Of lesser importance were the actual employment markets or the specifications of the job. The principal finding was that these test subjects expressed a particular feeling that the job would amount to more than money and that it was a demonstration of their "personal passions" (p. 87).

Wolniak and Pascarella (2007) conducted a study that used three groups of variables, independent and dependent, that totaled 14 variables explored. According to the results acquired from the statistical analyses of these variables' raw data, the researchers noted "that work college alumni consistently reported an advantage, and had greater overall satisfaction with their college experience" (p. 57). The researchers also noted that the work college alumni had a better understanding of the issues that surrounded their eventual placement in society, and it was surmised that this greater understanding had come through the more practical preparation afforded by a work college education. It was implied that the students were more mature and that the original decisions made, regarding career counseling, were predicated upon a more effective *prediction of career search behavior* because of a more practical and focused preparation in the work college environment.

Betz and Wolfe (2005) conducted their study from the dual perspective of research and the eventual development of a more accurate assessment instrument for use in the career counseling of graduating high school students and newly matriculated community college students. However, the researchers did not exactly find the results that they were expecting and they indicated that a better assessment instrument was necessary in order to predict career search and other behaviors in this studied, student population (p. 268). This suggested the need for a theoretical construct of a counseling instrument that would direct these students in the absence, or with minimal input from, counseling professionals with regard to career counseling and a career choice.

Patton and Creed (2007) indicated that one of the main purposes for their study was that "occupational aspirations in adolescents are useful predictors of later educational and occupational choices ... we need to understand more about occupational aspirations and expectations at various ages for the appropriate timing of career interventions for adolescents" (pp. 48-49). In their study, the researchers then used this idea in their exploration of the relationships between generally accepted, traditional variables, such as gender, and tied those variables to "key career behavioural [sic] constructs, namely career maturity, career goals and career indecision" (p. 49). The researchers found that there were significant associations between the traditional variables and the constructs, with relation to the prediction of career search behavior. There was a much larger success-oriented group, associated with the results of the sample, than could have been merely attributed to the percentage usually associated with chance. The resultant groupings were "(40 per cent of the skilled group, 52 percent of the semi-professional group, and 47 per cent of the professional group), which was a meaningful improvement on chance (of 33 per cent)" (p. 54).

Ganske and Ashby (2007) determined in their study that "in this study, we found that adaptive perfectionism also related to increased career decision-making self-efficacy" (p. 24). Further, in the publication of the study's results and discussion, the researchers mentioned that *prediction of career search behavior* does show a relationship to attributes such as self-esteem and adaptive perfectionism; data set groups that were explored in their study. However, the researchers did not complete the thought and stated that further research was necessary to determine adequate linkages (p. 26).

Blustein, Kenna, Gill, and Devoy (2008) determined that "clearly, more efforts are needed, both within the counseling profession and beyond, to create equal opportunities for people to access the resources needed for rewarding and sustainable work in the 21st century" (p. 306). Since the researchers did not find a suitable instrument in the literature survey and did not use one in their study, this suggested the need for a theoretical construct of a counseling instrument that would direct these students in the absence, or with minimal input from, counseling professionals with regard to career counseling and a career choice.

Fouad, Chen, Guillen, Henry, Kantemneni, Novacovic, Priester, and Terry (2007) found that since personal counseling was sometimes combined with career counseling, withdrawal from one adversely influenced the other. With regard to career search behavior, the researchers found that, "because career counseling clients are more likely to discontinue counseling earlier than those seeking personal counseling, they may lose the opportunity to explore both career and noncareer issues" (p. 21). This adverse linkage, as uncovered and discussed by the researchers, merited further investigation and the researchers suggested that it could be a subject for further research and study.

Duffy and Sedlacek (2007) determined that there were factors such as a family's income that was a factor in the prediction of the students' career search behavior. The students from middle income families chose social responsibility, with regard to a prospective career choice, whereas disadvantaged students and those from wealthy backgrounds chose factors such as high income (p. 361).

Gender

The results of empirical analysis and testing (Nauta, 2007) indicated, as had previously been demonstrated in a variety of published studies enumerated in the literature survey of her study, that gender did play a key role in the study of students with regard to eventual career counseling. She conclusively determined that, "consistent with previous research, significant differences were found for women and men on scores for realistic and investigative interests (men higher), realistic self-efficacy (men higher), neuroticism (women higher), and SE (women higher) ($ps < .05$)" (p. 169). Therefore, she did further investigations to determine what other issues or factors may have been extant for the relationships involved that fostered behavior that encouraged career search. In her first analysis, she determined that *year in school* and *gender* were adequate predictors, with regard to career search behavior. The net result was that in this type of study, gender as a variable became covariate with regard to the results of the statistical analysis of the resident sample in the study. Only a single self-efficacy type (artistic) was specifically shown to be exclusive to self-efficacy, regarding career choice, and this variable was also specifically tied to gender (p. 172).

Larson and Borgen (2006) concluded that gender, across the four samples of 1,173 students in the population analyzed, did not play a significant role with regard to "personality and confidence correlations" (p.301). Tang, Pan, and Newmeyer (2008) conducted a study that explored the relationships between various personality factors and the resulting relationships between those factors that developed into the making of career choices.

One of the variables that the researchers explored in their study was outcome expectation, as a personality factor that affected career decision aspirations, with its relationships to *gender*. The results of the study indicated that a factor, with a relationship between personality and *gender*, was the expected outcome. Intuitively, the reader would suspect that gender would play an issue in such a study and that the results of the study would have corroborated this expected result. Of the eight prospective outcomes studied, there was a particularly high positive correlation related directly to the clients' expected outcomes. It was demonstrated that expectations could play a large role when it came to the eventual decision-making process in the relationship between personality and the test pool subjects' *gender*. The study found that career choices were indeed very different, when it came to career selections and expectations, as categorized by personality factors with relation to *gender*.

Blustein, Kenna, Gill, and Devoy (2008) conclusively demonstrated that *gender* was an issue in career counseling and stated that significant support and effort were needed "to assist clients as they navigate the very real barriers to success that those who are not White, middle-class, male, and educated encounter as they search for work" (p. 302).

Fouad, Chen, Guillen, Henry, Kantemneni, Novacovic, Priester, and Terry (2007) conducted a variety of analyses on their data sample and concluded that there were *gender* differences, with regard to counseling, but "we did not find differences between men and women on values toward career counseling." Almost uniformly, women had better working relationships toward the counselor, "perceived the counselor as more attractive... and trustworthy." From the "holistic" sense, regarding the counseling, the *gender* perspective difference was statistically significant. With respect to *gender*, the test subjects held markedly different opinions concerning the counseling (but not the value of counseling as a whole) and its social implications (negative aspects of having any counseling at all). Men were more opposed to the counseling process in general, and women showed little predisposition for a negative outlook or "stigma" concerning the counseling process itself (p. 28).

Duffy and Sedlacek (2007) determined that *gender* did play a role in career counseling and the career choices made by students. The researchers found in their study, that "men were more likely to espouse extrinsic values, whereas women were more likely to espouse social values (p. 361). For their study, extrinsic values, in a prospective career position, were meant to be, for example, the high income element associated with the prospective position. Social values, on the other hand, were taken to mean social responsibility to humanity, or perhaps to the environment.

Year in school

Based upon information from her literature review in the published study, Nauta (2007) went on to study *year in school* as a factor and determined that the more advanced students engaged in behavior that lead to more exploration of career choices. Nauta's results indicated that the *year in school*, based upon empirical analysis of the data grounded in her study, was considered to be a variable that was covariate. Therefore, she did further investigations to determine what other issues or factors may have been extant for the relationships involved that fostered behavior that encouraged career search. In her first analysis, she determined that the *year in school* and *gender* were adequate predictors, with regard to career search behavior (p. 169).

Amir and Gati (2006) reported that those students who were more advanced in their respective programs of study, had less difficulty with career decision-making. Thus, the year in school was a factor in the decision making process and affected the students in the research sample. The students' eventual employment was predicated upon their immediate skill employed in the job search for a position after graduation.

Tang, Pan, and Newmeyer (2008) conducted a study that examined a test pool of subjects that were high school students. The *year in school* was one of the six variables in the first part of the study. It was found that the more mature the students were, as they neared graduation from high school, the more mature were their expectations and thus their career search expectations and their career search behavior.

Bloxom et al (2008) specifically studied grade 12 students because these were students in transition, and they would have a great need to pursue career counseling and career search behaviors. It was the researchers' rationale that these students would soon be graduated from high school, and the students would either need to find some employment or make decisions about further training (p. 91).

Wolniak and Pascarella (2007) conducted a study that used three groups of variables, independent and dependent, that totaled 14 variables explored. According to the results acquired from the statistical analyses of these variables' raw data, the researchers noted "that work college alumni consistently reported an advantage, and had greater overall satisfaction with their college experience" (p. 57). The researchers also noted that the work college alumni had a better understanding of the issues that surrounded their eventual placement in society. It was surmised that this greater understanding had come through the more practical preparation afforded by a work college education. With respect to a better understanding, the maturity of the students did correlate with the *year in school*, according to the researchers. It was implied that the students were more mature and that the original decisions made, regarding career counseling, were predicated upon the maturity level of the students and due to a more practical and focused preparation in the work college environment.

Moore et al., (2007) contended in their study that, "by definition, at-risk students will encounter problems in acculturation, achievement and retention once they enter the college environment" (p. 10). To follow up on this concept with the students, throughout the study, the researchers put into place graduated programs, based upon the *year in school*, to acculturate the students to the eventual attendance in, and progress in, the undergraduate college environment. The researchers contended that starting earlier in the high school curriculum, with acculturation programs for eventual college attendance for these disadvantaged students, improved the students' performance in the students' eventual college curriculum because of modified expectations and experience.

Betz and Wolfe (2005) addressed the recent school-to-work legislation (1994 to 2001) that has prompted a greater interest by researchers and scientists in the bridging of the high school to college population of students, who will enter the workspace earlier than traditional graduates. However, the researchers pointed out that there has been some neglect of the high school student population, that will not be college bound, and that these students also needed vocational and career counseling. The researchers determined that the year in school was significant and that it did bear upon the reliability of the assessment instruments utilized in their two studies. However, the results were not what they had expected and the *year in school* did not play as significant of a role in the determination of their results as originally planned. Other factors provided a greater influence on the mostly predictable nature of the results achieved by their studies (p. 253). The researchers hoped that further studies would be made, with regard to the foundation and use of an appropriate assessment instrument, for this subject population. This suggested the need for a theoretical construct of a counseling instrument that would direct these students in the absence of, or with minimal input from, counseling professionals with regard to career counseling and a career choice.

Patton and Creed (2007) determined in their study results that *year in school* was a factor, with regard to career counseling, because "there is a clear relationship between career maturity and occupational aspirations" (p. 56). Their results statement was based upon the intuitive original assumption that the more mature students, who were more advanced in the grades, would be more mature concerning their career counseling and career aspirations. The study merely brought this concept out in the achieved results, secondary to the principal objectives.

Use of testing instrument in Career Counseling:

The comparison of a paper instrument and an online career assessment

Miller (2007) reported that career counselors were not necessarily aware of the many assessment instruments that were available for career counseling. Miller further suggested, in order to be accurate about the selection process of an assessment instrument for use in the career counseling of clients, that the career "counselors need information on the technical quality of the measures (e.g., reliability, validity, appropriateness)" (pp. 14-15). The results of this study suggested that career counselors were not found to be as well trained as they could have been and that more training was needed in order to service the client population properly. Miller also found that there was a very high degree of congruence between the paper and online instruments used in his study. Miller suggested that more study needed to be performed, in addressing this particular client population, and that work needed to be done in the design of assessment instruments for career counseling. This suggested the need for a theoretical construct of a counseling instrument that would direct these students in the absence, or with minimal input from, counseling professionals with regard to career counseling and a career choice.

Tang, Pan, and Newmeyer (2008) used the Holland RIASEC model (a "paper" administered assessment instrument), in their testing of the subject test pool, as one of the assessment instruments for harvesting the data for their study. Since some of the other instruments were computer-actuated, and the results between the paper and computer assessment instruments were necessarily adjusted and made allowance for in the study, the results of the study were not adversely affected by the use of paper versus the computer to harvest raw data (p. 6).

Career Counseling (use of a testing instrument): Do they know what they're doing?

Harrington and Harrington (2007) stated in their study that, "counselors need to be sensitive to possible interpretation regarding an individual's self-efficacy beliefs." The researchers maintained that counselors sometimes failed to make the link between self-efficacy and personality, because the assessment instrument results didn't indicate an actual interest or talent to support the counseling client's perceived interest in a career (p. 27). This meant that the counselor didn't actually know what they were doing, when it came to what should have been considered effective career counseling of their clients. The researchers continued with the results that career counselors were not as successful as the reports have indicated, since the U.S. Census Bureau reported that 2 out of 3 high school graduates were uncertain about their own innate abilities or even which major or interest to pursue in college (p. 28). Bloxom et al (2008) found that grade 12 students were not impressed with current career counseling and that "they generally do not find current career planning resources to be very helpful" (p. 90).

Blustein, Kenna, Gill, and Devoy (2008) concluded that changes in the composition of the student population have moved counselors "beyond the confines of how they have been trained and may move them into unfamiliar and uncomfortable territory." Since the student composition of the population to be counseled has changed, the counseling process will continue to "disenfranchise clients" until there are more specific counseling and assessment tools to address their needs (p. 302). Since the population at risk was the student pool involved in work-based education, or school-to-work, this suggested the need for a theoretical construct of a counseling instrument that would direct these students in the absence, or with minimal input from, counseling professionals with regard to career counseling and a career choice.

Fouad, Chen, Guillen, Henry, Kantemneni, Nova-covic, Priester, and Terry (2007) found that men did not trust the counselor as much as women test subjects did. With attitudes exemplified and demonstrated by the test subjects, the results depicted by the researchers could be taken to mean that the test instruments were flawed, or that there were significant enough differences in gender responses to possibly suggest that the counselors either didn't have a competent grasp of their counseling responsibilities, or that the counselors just failed to follow through with adequate counseling results. This position is unclear in the results of the study, and it is evident that more study and research into this area are needed for a conclusive, clear result (p. 28).

Use of a testing instrument to establish personality for Career Counseling

Larson and Borgen (2006) concluded that the use of a testing instrument, as a practical implementation of theories and "best practices" in the career search, served to combine the best of the traits studied and explored. More specifically, those traits that concerned the career counseling would be self-efficacy, interests and personality (p. 308). Bloxom et al (2008) found, based upon testing instrument results and statistical correlation of those results, that almost half of the students in the test sample were confident. The students felt that they would be able to find a job that they enjoyed, a career that would eventually be suitable or be able to enroll in the career training that would help them to advance (after graduation from high school) (p.90).

Betz and Wolfe (2005) concluded in the results of their study that "to further research on the utility of parallel measures of self-efficacy and interests with high school students, including those who are not college bound, expanded means of measuring these parallel sets of constructs are needed" (p. 253). The researchers indicated that a better testing instrument, to establish personality for career counseling, was needed for the proper assessment of the students' personality and the direction of the students in this subject pool. Since the population at risk was the student pool involved in work-based education, or school-to-work, this suggested the need for a theoretical construct of a counseling instrument that would direct these students in the absence, or with minimal input from, counseling professionals with regard to career counseling and a career choice.

Patton and Creed (2007) determined that the use of the proper testing instrument, to establish personality for career counseling, was integral to their eventual findings. The researchers found that "sixty-two percent of students were classified successfully ... which was a meaningful improvement on chance allocation (which would have been 50 per cent/50 per cent)" (p. 51). Thus, the analysis of their raw data showed high, positive correlations, that were originally anticipated in their hypotheses (as an eventual result of the proper instruments' use), in the accompanying study of the proper testing instruments to determine personality for career counseling.

Ganske and Ashby (2007) maintained, in their study, that some particular assessment instruments (that establish personality for career counseling) were better (in some cases) than others, when they stated that "results from research using the APSR have demonstrated strong support for its psychometric integrity." Their main concern for the study was to produce reliable results concerning perfectionism, maladaptive versus adaptive, along with the emotional personality attributes that accompanied these frameworks. The researchers explored a variety of assessment instruments and conclusively stated that the instrument used does matter (p. 21).

Duffy and Sedlacek (2007) found that 47% of students sought careers that reflected career outcomes. Thus, the researchers determined that personality, and its related determinants, had a considerable impact upon choices made by students in the sample and those "values may have on decision making and their usefulness in conjunction with traditional measures of interests, skills, and personality" (p. 362). This gave considerable credence to the viewpoint that the use of a testing instrument to establish personality for career counseling was vital to the eventual success of those students examined in the sample. Since the sample was composed of 3,570 first year college students, and no mention was made of an incoming career assessment instrument that was tailored specifically to this population, this suggested the need for a theoretical construct of a counseling instrument that would direct these students in the absence of, or with minimal input from, counseling professionals with regard to career counseling and a career choice.

Social and economic conditions

Bloxom et al (2008) stated that a limitation of their study was that "socioeconomic status" was not involved in the testing or results. Thus, if socioeconomic status had been a factor, the results might have been somewhat different from those realized and published (p. 94). Wolniak and Pascarella (2007) conducted a study that used three groups of variables, independent and dependent, that totaled 14 variables explored. According to the results acquired from the statistical analyses of these variables' raw data, the researchers noted "that work college alumni consistently reported an advantage, and had greater overall satisfaction with their college experience" (p. 57). The researchers also noted that the work college alumni had a better understanding of the issues that surrounded their eventual placement in society and it was surmised that this greater understanding had come through the more practical preparation afforded by a work college education. It was expressly stated by the researchers, that the students who had come from disadvantaged backgrounds, concerning *social and economic conditions*, had received the greatest benefit from the nature of the practical and focused preparation afforded by the work college environment.

Moore et al., (2007) contended in their study that, "by definition, at-risk students will encounter problems in acculturation, achievement and retention once they enter the college environment" (p. 10). Throughout the study, the researchers put into place graduated programs, based upon the *social and economic conditions* of the students' background, to acculturate the students to the eventual attendance in, and progress in, the undergraduate college environment. The researchers contended that starting earlier in the high school curriculum, with acculturation programs for eventual college attendance for these disadvantaged students, improved the students' performance in that eventual college curriculum because of modified expectations and experience.

Patton and Creed (2007) conducted a study that evaluated a student sample of "333 high school students enrolled in Years 8-12 in one suburban school situated in a middle-level socioeconomic part of Brisbane, Australia" (p. 49). The researchers published results that indicated that "groups held high status aspirations and expectations, perhaps reflecting that these data were gathered from a school in a middle class socioeconomic area" (p. 56). Based upon this study, and the accompanying results achieved, the researchers concluded that socioeconomic status did matter and that it did contribute to the eventual findings derived from a critical study of their subject test pool.

Blustein, Kenna, Gill, and Devoy (2008) stated that individuals worked and expected to obtain, as a function of that work, "economic and social power" (p. 297). The particular student population that was addressed, in the study's test subject pool, was some school-to-work, as well as some disadvantaged students. As a result of the researchers' study, it was evident that the subject students, who were not well handled by the counseling system, were looking for more than just mere employment.

Duffy and Sedlacek (2007) determined that there were factors, such as a family's income, that were a factor in the prediction of the students' career search behavior. The students from middle income families chose income, with regard to a prospective career choice, whereas disadvantaged students, and those from wealthy backgrounds, chose factors such as prestige (p. 361).

Long term effects

Wolniak and Pascarella (2007) noted in their study that students, who were eventually graduated from work colleges, if they had come from disadvantaged environments or backgrounds, received the greatest *long term effects* benefit from a work college education and performed better, in a practical sense because of it. Moore et al., (2007) contended in their study that, "by definition, at-risk students will encounter problems in acculturation, achievement and retention once they enter the college environment" (p. 10). Throughout their study, the researchers put into place graduated programs, based upon the *social and economic conditions* of the students' background, to acculturate the students to the eventual attendance in, and progress during, the undergraduate college experience. This acculturation was supposed to alter the *long term effects* of being disadvantaged, and the problems associated with the accompanying lack of experience, on the part of the students in the subject test pool. The researchers contended that starting earlier in the high school curriculum, with acculturation programs for eventual college attendance for these disadvantaged students, improved the students' performance in that eventual college curriculum because of modified expectations and experience.

Patton and Creed (2007) conducted a study that related that, "occupational aspirations and expectations have been viewed as significant determinants of both short-term educational and long-term career choices" (p. 47). Secondary to the findings published in their results of that study, the researchers mentioned that the *long-term effects* were in part attributable to the occupational aspirations and expectations experienced by adolescents. This occurred as the adolescents entered the career search phase of career counseling to determine career search and choice frameworks.

Role induction

Fouad, Chen, Guillen, Henry, Kantemneni, Novacovic, Priester, and Terry (2007) found that the application of three different methods of role induction changed the overall perceptions of career counseling among the test subjects in their study sample. A principal purpose of the research study was to determine if role induction altered the perceptions of the test subjects' views toward career counseling. The researchers found that gender played an important role in the determination of attitudes toward career counseling and that the methods of role induction provided important insight into the career counseling process. However, the researchers indicated that more study was necessary, to conclusively determine the value of the selected three methods of role induction, and that future studies should more completely control for gender in the original sampling harvest of data (p. 24).

Duffy and Sedlacek (2007) determined that "the data indicate that a focus on work values in career counseling may be useful for many incoming 1st-year college students." Thus, role induction, or the definition of a prospective work role through the induction of, and the use of, work values, was of considerable benefit (taken in perspective). The judicious application of role induction was useful as a career counseling tool, but the researchers indicated that more research was needed in this particular area (p. 363).

Depth Summary

Concerning career interests and vocational confidence, there were a number of findings. Nauta (2007) maintained that career interests and vocational confidence were not mutually exclusive and her research demonstrated a conclusive link between career interests and vocational confidence. Amir and Gati (2006) found that there were some important correlations between factors that influenced the degree of vocational confidence and that there was a profound difference between them. Bloxom et al (2008) noted that approximately 80% of students felt that a career that required post-secondary education or training was important. Moore et al., (2007) discussed the positive results, concerning a multiple year program that promoted and developed incoming college students who hailed from sub-economic backgrounds, and the program was designed to work on the practical aspects of vocational confidence through a series of assessment instruments and sub-programs that taught learning by "doing" to the students. Betz and Wolfe (2005) determined, based upon the two studies that the researchers performed, that there was a vast difference between intentions and probable, actual behavior.

Patton and Creed (2007) found that students who held different RIASEC aspirations to expectations were correspondingly more career indecisive, held expectations for lower status jobs, had lower self-esteem, held lower career goals and exhibited a poorer career development attitude, than their non-discrepant peers. Ganske and Ashby (2007) determined that when interests manifested themselves in the decision-making process, and when the interests' related strength was utilized (perceived as vocational confidence), that the resulting career counseling process changed and better choices were evidently made. Duffy and Sedlacek (2007) determined that students were divided along specific lines when the aspects of career interests and vocational confidence were considered.

Fouad, Chen, Guillen, Henry, Kantemneni, Novacovic, Priester, and Terry (2007) determined that students were not content with the specific counseling received during the career counseling process, and that there were significant amounts of career interest concerns among the test subject population. Blustein, Kenna, Gill and Devoy (2008) determined that those students, who were from disadvantaged backgrounds, were also the students who did not have access to formalized counseling and that these were not the types of students that professionals addressed in professional discussions. The results of these two studies suggested a concern that will be addressed in the Application segment - the theoretical construct of a counseling instrument that would direct these students in the absence, or with minimal input from, counseling professionals with regard to career counseling and a career choice.

There were some conclusive findings with regard to self-efficacy and personality. Nauta (2007) concluded that only a single self-efficacy type (artistic) was specifically shown to be exclusive to self-efficacy, regarding career choice, and that this variable was also specifically tied to gender. She explained that factors associated with self-efficacy and personality were not a part of the search behavior of students, once they started to examine prospective environments for work. Larson and Borgen

(2006) specifically stated that their results showed that personality mattered tremendously in many aspects of career self-efficacy. Their study showed a link, positively correlated as a result of the results from that study, that there was a positive linkage between self-efficacy and personality.

Harrington and Harrington (2007) found that career counselors were not as successful as the reports had previously indicated. Amir and Gati (2006) found that there was a strong correlation between self-efficacy and the personality elements involved in career decision making skills. The students' comprehension and overall understanding of the process, along with the use of their personality elements, had a significant impact upon their career decision making self-efficacy. Tang, Pan, and Newmeyer (2008) demonstrated that expectations played a large role, when it came to the eventual decision-making process, in the relationship between personality and the students' eventual, career decision-making self-efficacy.

Betz and Wolfe (2005) indicated that males correspondingly did better in the mechanical aspects of career-based personality attributes, whereas females performed better in the helping and cultural sensitivity personality attributes. Patton and Creed (2007) characterized the relationship between self-efficacy and personality in a new manner, when they explicitly stated that the self-efficacy construct, or self-concept, was represented as self-esteem. The re-characterization worked, because the researchers had strong, positive data correlation among the variables when these traits were collected and interpreted as self-esteem. Ganske and Ashby (2007) stated that it was the career counselor's obligation to improve the client's self-efficacy, in order to facilitate appropriate responses to counseling and effectively use personality attributes to make eventual career decisions.

There were some specific findings with regard to the prediction of career search behavior. Nauta (2007) determined that year in school was an adequate predictor, with regard to career search behavior. Larson and Borgen (2006) found a framework for the remainder of the extant behaviors, which characterized the career search in particular: career interests and self-efficacy, career development, career choice, job performance, and job satisfaction. Amir and Gati (2006) reported that students' eventual employment was predicated upon their immediate skill employed in the job search for a position after graduation.

Tang, Pan, and Newmeyer (2008) demonstrated that expectations played a large role in the eventual decision-making process, with regard to the relationship between personality and the prediction of career search behavior. Bloxom et al (2008) found that their test subjects expressed a particular feeling that the eventual job that these subjects took would amount to more than just money; it was a demonstration of their personal passions. Wolniak and Pascarella (2007) found, in their research sample, that the students were more mature and that the original decisions made, regarding career counseling, were predicated upon a more effective prediction of career search behavior. These results were attributed to a more practical and focused preparation due to the work college environment background.

Betz and Wolfe (2005) did not exactly find the results

that they had expected, and they indicated that a better assessment instrument was needed in order to predict career search, and other behaviors, in their student population. This suggested the need for a theoretical construct of a counseling instrument that would direct these students in the absence, or with minimal input from, counseling professionals with regard to career counseling and a career choice.

Patton and Creed (2007) indicated that occupational aspirations in adolescents were useful predictors of later educational and occupational choices. However, more understanding was needed, concerning occupational aspirations and expectations at the various ages, for the appropriate timing of career interventions for adolescents to be timely. Ganske and Ashby (2007) determined that the prediction of career search behavior does show a relationship to attributes, such as self-esteem and adaptive perfectionism; data set groups that were explored in their study. However, the researchers did not complete the thought and stated that further research was necessary to determine adequate linkages.

Blustein, Kenna, Gill, and Devoy (2008) did not find a suitable instrument in the literature survey and did not use one in their study. This suggested the need for a theoretical construct of a counseling instrument that would direct students in the absence, or with minimal input from, counseling professionals with regard to career counseling and a career choice. Fouad, Chen, Guillen, Henry, Kantemneni, Novacovic, Priester, and Terry (2007) found that since personal counseling was sometimes combined with career counseling, withdrawal from one adversely influenced the other. This adverse linkage, as uncovered and discussed by the researchers, merited further investigation and could be a subject for further research and study. Duffy and Sedlacek (2007) determined that there were factors, such as a family's income, that were interceding factors in the prediction of the students' career search behavior.

There were some specific results found with regard to gender. Nauta (2007) indicated that gender, as a variable, became covariate with regard to the results of the statistical analysis of the resident sample in her study. Only a single self-efficacy type (artistic) was specifically shown to be exclusive to self-efficacy regarding career choice and this variable was also specifically tied to gender. Larson and Borgen (2006) concluded that gender did not play a significant role with regard to personality and confidence correlations. Tang, Pan, and Newmeyer (2008) found that career choices were indeed very different, when it came to career selections and expectations, as categorized by personality factors with relation to gender.

Blustein, Kenna, Gill, and Devoy (2008) conclusively demonstrated that gender was an issue in career counseling and stated that significant support and effort were needed to assist clients, as the clients navigated the very real barriers to success that those who are not White, middle-class, male, and educated encounter, as they search for work. Fouad, Chen, Guillen, Henry, Kantemneni, Novacovic, Priester, and Terry (2007) concluded, with respect to gender, that the test subjects held markedly different opinions concerning career counseling (but not the value of counseling as a whole) and its social implications (negative aspects of having any counseling at all). Men were more opposed to the counseling process in general, and women showed little predisposition for a negative outlook or stigma concerning the counseling process itself. Duffy and Sedlacek (2007) determined that gender does play a role in career counseling and career choices made by students.

There were some specific results found with regard to the year in school. Nauta (2007) determined that *year in school* and *gender* were adequate predictors, with regard to career search behavior. Amir and Gati (2006) reported that, concerning year in school, the students' eventual employment would be predicated upon their immediate skill employed in the job search for a position after graduation. Tang, Pan, and Newmeyer (2008) found that the more mature students were, as they neared graduation from high school, the more mature were their expectations and thus their career search expectations (along with their career search behavior).

Bloxom et al (2008) specifically studied grade 12 students because these were students in transition and the students had a great need to pursue career counseling and career search behaviors. It was the researchers' rationale that these students would soon be graduated from high school, and would either need to find some employment or make decisions about further training. Wolniak and Pascarella (2007) stated, with regard to year in school, that their students, in the test sample, were more mature and that the original decisions made, regarding career counseling, were predicated upon the maturity level of those students and were due to a more practical and focused preparation afforded in the work college environment.

Moore et al., (2007) contended that starting earlier in

the high school curriculum, with acculturation programs for eventual college attendance for disadvantaged students, improved the students' performance in that eventual college curriculum because of modified expectations and experience. Betz and Wolfe (2005) determined that the year in school was significant and did bear upon the reliability of the assessment instruments utilized in their two studies. The researchers suggested the need for a theoretical construct of a counseling instrument that would direct these students in the absence of, or with minimal input from, counseling professionals with regard to career counseling and a career choice. Patton and Creed (2007) determined in their study results, that year in school was a factor, with regard to career counseling, because there was a clear relationship between career maturity and occupational aspirations.

There were some specific results found, with regard to the use of a testing instrument in career counseling. Concerning the comparison of a paper instrument and an online career assessment, Miller (2007) reported that there was a very high degree of congruence between the paper and online instruments used in his study. Miller suggested that work needed to be done in the design of assessment instruments for career counseling. This suggested the need for a theoretical construct of a counseling instrument that would direct students in the absence of, or with minimal input from, counseling professionals with regard to career counseling and a career choice. Tang, Pan, and Newmeyer (2008) indicated that the results, between the paper and computer assessment instruments, were necessarily adjusted and made allowance for, in their study. The results of their study were not adversely affected by the use of paper versus the computer to harvest raw data.

Concerning the use of a career counseling (testing instrument) and whether counselors know what they're doing, Harrington and Harrington (2007) stated in their study that career counselors were not as successful as the reports had previously indicated, since the U.S. Census Bureau reported that 2 out of 3 high school graduates were uncertain about their own innate abilities, or even which major or interest to pursue in college. Bloxom et al (2008) found that grade 12 students were not impressed with current career counseling, and that they generally did not find current career planning resources to be very helpful.

Blustein, Kenna, Gill, and Devoy (2008) concluded that, since the student composition of the population to be counseled has changed, the counseling process will continue to disenfranchise clients until there were more specific counseling and assessment tools to address their needs. This suggested the need for a theoretical construct of a counseling instrument that would direct these students in the absence, or with minimal input from, counseling professionals with regard to career counseling and a career choice. Fouad, Chen, Guillen, Henry, Kantemneni, Novacovic, Priester, and Terry (2007) found that there were significant enough differences in gender responses, to possibly suggest that the counselors either didn't have a competent grasp of their counseling responsibilities or that the counselors just failed to follow through with adequate counseling results.

Concerning the use of a testing instrument to establish personality for career counseling, Larson and Borgen

(2006) concluded that almost half of the students in their test sample were confident that they would be able to find a job that they enjoyed, a career that would be suitable or be able to enroll in the career training that would help them to advance (after graduation from high school). Betz and Wolfe (2005) concluded that further research, on the utility of parallel measures of self-efficacy and interests with high school students, including those who were not college bound (expanding the means of measuring those parallel sets of constructs), was needed. This suggested the need for a theoretical construct of a counseling instrument that would direct these students in the absence, or with minimal input from, counseling professionals with regard to career counseling and a career choice.

Patton and Creed (2007) determined that the use of the proper testing instrument, to establish personality for career counseling, was integral to their eventual findings. The analysis of their raw data showed high, positive correlations in the accompanying study of the proper testing instruments, and properly determined personality for career counseling. Ganske and Ashby (2007) maintained, after exploring a variety of assessment instruments (in their study), that the instrument used for career counseling does matter.

Duffy and Sedlacek (2007) found that the use of a testing instrument to establish personality for career counseling could be vital to the eventual success of students. Since the sample was composed of 3,570 first year college students and no mention was made of an incoming career assessment instrument that was tailored specifically to this population, this suggested the need for a theoretical construct of a counseling instrument that would direct these students in the absence of, or with minimal input from, counseling professionals with regard to career counseling and a career choice.

With regard to social and economic conditions, Bloxom et al (2008) stated that a limitation of their study was that "socioeconomic status" was not involved in the testing or results. Wolniak and Pascarella (2007) found that students, who came from disadvantaged backgrounds, concerning social and economic conditions, received the greatest benefit from the nature of the practical and focused preparation provided in the work college environment. Moore et al., (2007) contended that, starting earlier in the high school curriculum, with acculturation programs for eventual college attendance for these disadvantaged students, improved the students' performance in that eventual college curriculum because of modified expectations and experience.

Patton and Creed (2007) concluded that socioeconomic status did matter, and that it did contribute to the eventual findings derived from a critical study of their subject test pool. Blustein, Kenna, Gill, and Devoy (2008) stated that the students, who were not well handled by the counseling system, were looking for more than mere employment. Duffy and Sedlacek (2007) determined that there were factors, such as a family's income, that were factors in the prediction of the students' career search behavior. The students from middle income families chose income, with regard to a prospective career choice, whereas disadvantaged students and those from wealthy backgrounds chose factors such as prestige.

Concerning long term effects, Wolniak and Pascarella (2007) noted in their study that students who were eventually graduated from work colleges, if they had come from disadvantaged environments or backgrounds, received the greatest long term effects benefit from the work college education and performed better, in a practical sense, because of it. Moore et al., (2007) contended that, starting earlier in the high school curriculum, with acculturation programs for eventual college attendance for these disadvantaged students, improved the students' performance in the eventual college curriculum because of modified expectations and experience. Patton and Creed (2007) found that the long-term effects were in part attributable to the occupational aspirations and expectations experienced by adolescents, as they entered the career search phase of career counseling, to determine career search and choice frameworks.

With regard to role induction, Fouad, Chen, Guillen, Henry, Kantemneni, Novacovic, Priester, and Terry (2007) found that the application of three different methods of role induction did change the overall perceptions of career counseling among the test subjects in their study. Duffy and Sedlacek (2007) determined that role induction could be used as a career counseling tool, but the researchers indicated that more research was needed in this particular area.

APPLICATION
Introduction

To discuss the knowledge requirements necessary to undertake the programming of a psychological test instrument for practical use in career counseling of the prospective college students in transition to a junior college or work college institution, there must first be some mention of the prerequisite items that form a framework for discussion. These items are the precursors to the beginning of such a discussion. McConnell (2004b) discussed some of the more pertinent areas that might be addressed in the framework for such a discussion. For example, if the use of seasoned, professional talent was assumed, there was the elementary point to the framework discussion that assessed an expert to be someone who had memorized "50,000 chunks of information." There was something of a dilemma concerning this assumed requirement, when it concerned the world of computing and software design. If a traditional expert, in another field, was usually considered to have to taken over ten years to amass such a wealth of knowledge to even be considered an expert, then there was something of an issue associated with this assumption with regard to computing. It was reported that half of the requisite knowledge to write computer software went out of date in less than three years. This consideration was what was referred to as "technology-related knowledge" (p. 37).

Accidental versus essential computing properties

McConnell (2004b) proposed a solution to this dichotomous observation, concerning the programming of software to meet particular needs. He stated that Fred Brooks published results in the late 1980's, that described a particular difference between the essentials necessary to engineer software and the transient technical aspects associated with the use of a particular software coding language that would quickly, in just a few short years, become obsolete. McConnell mentioned that Brooks' work centered upon two principal concepts, known as "*essence* and *accident*" (p. 38).

McConnell (2004b) noted that these terms had a somewhat different meaning, with regard to the concepts and framework of computing, as opposed to what might have been considered to be conventional usage in regular society. An *essential* property was something that made something, by definition, to be what it was. For example, an automobile requires tires to be functional, so then the tires would be considered to be an *essential*. However, if an automobile had an automatic, over-drive transmission, versus a manual transmission, this would be considered to be an *accidental* property. The transmission was still important to the functionality of the automobile, but the nature of what it was in particular, was not *essential*. This was how McConnell considered the computing framework to be a workable proposition over the long-term. The *accidental* knowledge (and thus the expertise continuation), on behalf of the software engineers and computer programmers, overcame the short-run, debilitating technological loss attributed to the software's obsolescence. Although the technical aspects became obsolete in only a few short years, it was the tenets of the *accidental* properties (concerning computing and software design), that actually made computer work possible at all. It was these *accidental* properties of software and engineering knowledge that overcame the mercurial nature of the *essential* properties (p. 38).

Complexity, conformity, changeability, and invisibility

There were several other considerations, with regard to the overall framework, which played a role in the engineering and programming of applications software. McConnell (2004b) mentioned these various aspects of the framework, and discussed them briefly. The considerations that could develop were known to be "*complexity, conformity, changeability, and invisibility.*" Since computing programs were considerably more complex than other things could be in society, there was a consideration that came to bear, even when a particular software language that exactly met all needs for the solution was found, and was applied to the problem at hand. *Complexity* was what resulted when all of the *accidental* considerations were removed from the framework. What became left over was then known to be the remaining *essentials.* Even when a suitable piece of software to serve the actual solution was employed, the software language was incredibly complex, the problems of applications still existed, when it came to the definition of the understanding of the coding and the adaptation of the code to concerns that existed in the actual world (pp. 38-39).

Another consideration, that was an integral part of the *complexity* discussion, was a further part of this original discussion. McConnell (2004b) contended that the *complexity* discussion gave rise to a discussion that centered upon *conformity*. Software that was written for practical use, needed to "*conform* to messy real-world constraints such as pre-existing hardware, third-party components, government regulations, business rules, and legacy data formats" (p. 39).

There was another difficulty that could really have an adverse effect upon the eventual software programming solution. McConnell (2004b) described *changeability* as an extremely difficult problem to overcome, with regard to software solutions. As software was used, if the software was a particularly useful piece of software, the users would get comfortable with it and then attempt to adapt the software package to other uses. Some of these applications were not within the purview of what the original developers had intended, so there came to be a number of "adaptations" that were necessary to keep the software functional. The more the changes were used, the more of these adaptations would be necessary and this further complicated the use of such software as the changes occurred (pp. 38-39).

The last consideration for the framework involved a consideration that may not have been usually considered to be an issue. McConnell (2004b) contended that software had a quality that was basically known as *invisibility*. Since software really couldn't be observed or understood very well in some contexts, through the use of "2-D or 3D geometric models," conventional attempts by the engineers and programmers to depict the order of the modules or commands then became ridiculously outlandish and difficult. Intuitively, the reader may find this to be true, if the reader has ever attempted to formulate a computer chart that showed the logic trail of a computer program or programming package. Thus, McConnell stated that considerable improvement had already been made with regard to the *accidental* parts of programming. The real work to be done remained, however, in improving the previously discussed *essential* elements of the framework known as, "*complexity, conformity, changeability, and invisibility*" (p. 39).

Size is important

A further consideration, regarding the construction of a piece of software, was the inherent size of the program itself. McConnell (2004a) put forth that there was a considerable bit of difference between, for example, a program that had 25,000 lines of code and a program that contained 250,000 lines of code. One might assume that the difficulties were simply a multiple of the number of lines of code. This would be the intuitive answer. However, in actuality, 250,000 lines were not ten times more difficult than 25,000 lines of code. Instead of a factor of ten, if there were ten times as many lines of code as in this particular example, "it probably implies 25 times as much construction and 40 times as much architecture and system testing" (p. 649).

There was also a factor associated with the number of programmers who worked on the project. McConnell (2004a) described the situation, regarding the size of the project, as it related to communications among the programmers. The theory that was applied, with regard to the communications concern as a function of the number of programmers, related to the number of paths between the various people who worked as programmers on the project. The larger the number of people who worked on the project, the more convoluted became the paths of the communications between all of the programmers. This could mean that the project became more difficult to complete, and that the number of conceivable errors would be multiplied, due to the tremendous amount of increased input that was applied to the programming project. For example, McConnell related that, "of projects that have 50 or more programmers have at least 1,200 potential paths. The more communication paths you have, the more time you spend communicating and the more opportunities are created for communication mistakes" (p. 650).

Concerning the time allocated and allotted to the actual steps of the project, the size of the project, with regard to the number of lines of computer code, had a dramatic influence upon how much time was spent on each step of the development activities. McConnell (2004a) realized that on a smaller project, one in the range of 8,000 to 10,000 lines of computer code, about two-thirds of the overall time spent on the project was spent upon construction of the software program. Only about five percent of the total time allocated was actually spent on preliminary planning aspects associated with "architecture and requirements" (pp. 654-655).

The twelve steps

A software project, regardless of the size considerations, must have a logical order of steps to be followed so that it will eventually become complete. McConnell (1998) detailed a variety of considerations, and all one dozen of those considerations play an important role in our prospective piece of psychological and career counseling software's completion. McConnell detailed these steps and, in order to promote success of the software project, they should be followed and completed in the appropriate order. The twelve steps are, "Requirements updates; Detailed design; Construction; Test case creation; User documentation updates; Technical reviews; Defect corrections; Technical coordination; Risk management; Project tracking; Integration and release; and End-of-stage wrap-up" (p 175).

McConnell (1998) detailed a variety of principal considerations that applied to each of the one-dozen steps of the software creation process and a brief synopsis follows, which will be extremely useful later in this Application segment to answer rhetorical questions related to usage and delivery. The updates of the software requirements are important because increased understanding occurs, on the part of the programmers and project managers, as the project itself unfolds. So, although the requirements were supposedly understood at the beginning of the process, "changing market conditions, and other factors may necessitate changes to requirements" (p. 176).

Designing something is not always straight-forward. McConnell (1998) noted that, although the writers block out what the design should look like, the eventual writing of the software code could alter the original plan somewhat with regard to how the system itself handles the various code commands. Thus, when designing the project's architecture, "if detailed design work uncovers flaws in the architecture, the project team revises the architecture using change control procedure" (p. 176). The construction of the code was probably the most continuous portion of the 12 steps. If someone created a systematic architecture, and then created the code based upon it, then there would be a minimum number of issues associated with this particular step in the process. This particular situation can result, due to the fact that the "developer who creates the detailed design for a specific part of the software also writes the code for that part" (p. 176).

Part of eventual error testing is supported in the testing step. McConnell (1998) explained that when programmers were coding a particular stage of development, with regard to the lines of code, there should be a "full set of test cases needed to test the functionality developed during the stage" (p. 176). In other words, no administrator or programmer could sign off on the coding, stating that the code was complete, unless a specific module of code had been tested with the associated set of test cases to show that the code module was indeed actually error-free. The user documentation updates should be performed in line with the other construction activities, according to the stage of development, in order to keep pace with the mountain of paperwork that develops during software design and construction. Although, as in the requirements update step, the coders and managers originally knew what was required, conditions during the coding and construction process have changed. That means that the "requirements specification" and "user manual" must also be updated, as the computer code is constructed, in a changed manner, from the original requirements specifications. This actually makes the software development flow easier and more predictably in the long-run, if the team updates the documents as the code is developed, written and tested. In this way, the information is fresh in everyone's mind and an accurate user manual is available to eventually distribute with the completed software package (p. 176).

In the development cycle associated with software, in this particular case a psychological piece of software to be used as an assessment instrument for career counseling, there is a step that involves a review. McConnell (1998) mentioned that a "technical review" should involve the people who developed a piece of software. Of the two different types of reviews, coding and designing, it would be difficult to determine which type of review would be more important. However, the principals should be involved with both types of review in that both reviews occur after the "post-architecture period," and both types of review generally involve the principals of both teams (who actually worked on the project). The important concept to realize in this part of the discussion is not the obvious statements concerning the fact that both reviews should occur. The important thing to remember is that the overall development plan should allow time to be budgeted for both of these reviews in order to promote the success of the project in totality (p. 177).

A continuing step in the overall process is the correction of errors in the program architecture, or in the code itself. McConnell (1998) maintained that a software project should only be allowed to continue to completion with the inherent stipulation that intermediate testing of the various steps or modules of code should occur after each step is completed. In other words, the developers should compel the programmers to make certain that the code is error free at the conclusion of each stage of the process of development, instead of waiting until the end of development to see if the software is functional. It would be important to perform verification at each step of the process, to make certain that the errors exposed by testing were corrected, before the next step of the process was allowed to begin. In this manner, a higher quality of the final product (the piece of software) could be realized by the developers (p. 177).

The coordination of any project can be important, but it can be extremely important concerning the development of specialized software. McConnell (1998) directed that if the preceding steps discussed to this point were followed, then the amount of "technical coordination" would be minimized. However, this technical coordination step is a step that should be budgeted, with regard to time allocation in the development cycle, in order to make certain that the project concludes on schedule with enough practically useful code to actually be released. Different groups should meet concerning a project of considerable size. The main concern was that the developers should be available to the coders, who should be available to the technical writers who write the user manuals, who should be available to the administrators to discuss scheduling. As mentioned in a previous step, the more people who are involved in the overall project, the more the pathways of communication that are eventually involved and the more convoluted the process can become (inviting errors of all types) (p. 177).

There can be a number of risks involved with software

development. McConnell (1998) even contended that "stage planning should be risk driven." Administrators should proceed with caution, and review the risk assessment lists, on a periodic basis, to determine if the risks were being adequately addressed and whether those risks were being minimized or even eliminated. As with the other steps that have been mentioned previously, risks change. Risk can evolve as the project evolves, due to a number of factors: requirements updates; design changes; user changes; and other considerations not foreseen at the onset of the project (p. 177).

As with project management fundamentals, there should be some sort of mechanism available to track the progress of the software project's evolution. There are a number of software packages that are commercially available that track tasks and task sub-sets, in addition to Project Management Professional software, that would allow administrators to track the progress of a software project.

This particular step may seem to be something of a re-statement of a previous step, but it is actually an independent step unto itself. McConnell (1998) suggested that there should be a step in the development process wherein the software project should be in what's known to be a "releasable state." In other words, the project should be able to stand alone. The piece of software should be able to be combined, from separate modules and pieces of code, for such a release. However, the release should be considered carefully from a business standpoint. Should the release be to the development partners, the end-user, or just other project managers for software evaluation? The list of possibilities might be endless, so this is something that should have been a decision in place before the project was started, in order to eliminate confusion and unwarranted arguing at the conclusion of the project. An important consideration, regardless of to which particular level the software package is actually released, is quality coordination. The "quality assurance group" should always get the final edition of the software to look at the parsing, help desk hints and module functions to approve a functional edition for an ultimate release to the end-user or customer (p. 178).

All things eventually conclude, regardless of the eventual outcome of the project. McConnell (1998) concluded that a software project needed an "end-of-stage wrap-up," in order to examine what went well for the project and what didn't. Further, this would be a last chance effort to adjust for any changes to the overall direction of the project. This final step also provided a development tool to save time on future projects, by looking at the steps that went well, and those that didn't, in order to set in place workable frameworks for future projects. If the adage that *time is money* is still accurate, this wrap-up is a good tool to employ in order to save time and money on future projects by adjusting for those tasks that were poorly accomplished on the present software development project (p. 179).

Recapitulation and the software package choice

Of the considerations, with regard to the choice of software package for an application, a short recapitulation is in order. McConnell (2004b) mentioned various aspects of the software framework, and discussed them briefly. The considerations that could develop were known to be *"complexity, conformity, changeability, and invisibility."* Since computing programs were considerably more complex than other things could be in society, there was a consideration that came to bear, even when a particular software language that exactly met all needs for the solution was found, and was applied to the problem at hand. *Complexity* was what resulted when all of the *accidental* considerations were removed from the framework. What became left over was then known to be the remaining *essentials*. Even when a suitable piece of software to serve the actual solution was employed, the software language was incredibly complex, the problems of applications still existed, when it came to the definition of the understanding of the coding and the adaptation of the code to concerns that existed in the actual world (pp. 38-39). Excel could be used to address these considerations, when used to program an applications package for counseling.

Another consideration, that was an integral part of the *complexity* discussion, was a further part of this original discussion. McConnell (2004b) contended that the *complexity* discussion gave rise to a discussion that centered upon *conformity*. Software that was written for practical use, needed to *"conform* to messy real-world constraints such as pre-existing hardware, third-party components, government regulations, business rules, and legacy data formats" (p. 39). Excel could be used to address these considerations, when used to program an applications package for counseling. Excel could conform to many types of environments, due to the fact that it is simply a spreadsheet of line item statements. Excel is a logical progression, with regard to coding and execution.

There was another difficulty that could really have an adverse effect upon the eventual software programming solution. McConnell (2004b) described *changeability* as an extremely difficult problem to overcome, with regard to software solutions. As software was used, if the software was a particularly useful piece of software, the users would get comfortable with it and then attempt to adapt the software package to other uses. Some of these applications were not within the purview of what the original developers had intended, so there came to be a number of "adaptations" that were necessary to keep the software functional. The more the changes were used, the more of these adaptations would be necessary and this further complicated the use of such software as the changes occurred (pp. 38-39). Excel could be used to address these considerations, when used to program an applications package for counseling. The software can be re-written on demand, and is very changeable.

The last consideration for the framework involved a consideration that may not have been usually considered to be an issue. McConnell (2004b) contended that software had a quality that was basically known as *invisibility*. Since software really couldn't be observed or understood very well in some contexts, through the use of "2-D or 3D geometric models," conventional attempts by the engineers and programmers to depict the order of the modules or commands then became ridiculously outlandish and difficult. Intuitively, the reader may find this to be true, if the reader ever attempted to formulate a computer chart that showed the logic trail of a computer program or programming package. Thus, McConnell stated that considerable improvement had already been made with regard to the *accidental* parts of programming. The real work to be done remained, however, in improving the previously discussed essential elements of the framework known as, *"complexity, conformity, changeability, and invisibility"* (p. 39). Excel could be used to address these considerations, when used to program an applications package for counseling. Although it is invisible, just like other software packages, the continued use of Excel makes many of the copy and paste coding functions relatively easy for the coder and user. Excel is very easy to observe, understand and use (for and by the end-user) (Brown, 1999).

A further consideration, regarding the construction of a piece of software, is the inherent size of the program itself. McConnell (2004a) put forth that there was a considerable bit of difference between, for example, a program that had 25,000 lines of code and a program that contained 250,000 lines of code. One might assume that the difficulties were simply a multiple of the number of lines of code. This would be the intuitive answer. However, in actuality, 250,000 lines were not ten times more difficult than 25,000 lines of code. Instead of a factor of ten, if there were ten times as many lines of code as in this particular example, "it probably implies 25 times as much construction and 40 times as much architecture and system testing" (p. 649). Excel could be used to address these considerations, when used to program an applications package for counseling. Brown (1999) directed that this consideration could be easily addressed by being able to create "templates." In other words, by "creating a workbook, you can always "clone" it to create a new one. You open it, save it with a different name, and then plug in new values" (p. 54). A larger size doesn't necessarily mean more effective usage. The re-useability of the code makes Excel a sound choice for counseling software creation, in this particular application.

There was also a factor associated with the number of programmers who worked on the project. McConnell (2004a) described the situation, regarding the size of the project, as it related to communications among the programmers. The theory that was applied, with regard to the communications concern as a function of the number of programmers, related to the number of paths between the various people who worked as programmers on the project. The larger the number of people who worked on the project, the more convoluted became the paths of the communications between all of the programmers. This could mean that the project became more difficult to complete, and that the number of conceivable errors would be multiplied, due to the tremendous amount of increased input that was applied to the programming project. For example, McConnell related that, "of projects that have 50 or more programmers have at least 1,200 potential paths. The more communication paths you have, the more time you spend communicating and the more opportunities are created for communication mistakes" (p. 650). This is exceptionally easy to solve with Excel. Only one person, because of the simplicity of the code and the coding process, needs to program the counseling software. This virtually eliminates the communications issues involved with the large number of coders and designers concern.

Concerning the time allocated and allotted to the actual steps of the project, the size of the project, with regard to the number of lines of computer code, had a dramatic influence upon how much time was spent on each step of the development activities. McConnell (2004a) realized that on a smaller project, one in the range of 8,000 to 10,000 lines of computer code, about two-thirds of the overall time spent on the project was spent upon construction of the software program. Only about five percent of the total time allocated was actually spent on preliminary planning aspects associated with "architecture and requirements" (pp. 654-655). This is a non-issue for Excel programs, since these programs generally only involve a few hundred lines of code (or less) (Brown, 1999).

A software project, regardless of the size considerations, must have a logical order of steps to be followed so that it will eventually become complete. McConnell (1998) detailed a variety of considerations, and all one dozen of those considerations play an important role in our prospective piece of psychological and career counseling software's completion. McConnell detailed these steps and, in order to promote success of the software project, they should be followed and completed in the appropriate order. The twelve steps are, "Requirements updates; Detailed design; Construction; Test case creation; User documentation updates; Technical reviews; Defect corrections; Technical coordination; Risk management; Project tracking; Integration and release; and End-of-stage wrap-up" (p 175). These steps can also be used in the development of an Excel program, but many of them, due to the nature of Excel, are either shortened or are virtually eliminated - they sometimes become a moot point (Brown, 1999).

McConnell (1998) detailed a variety of principal considerations that applied to each of the one-dozen steps of the software creation process and a brief synopsis follows, which will be extremely useful later in this application segment to answer rhetorical questions related to usage and delivery. The updates of the software requirements are important because increased understanding occurs, on the part of the programmers and project managers, as the project itself unfolds. So, although the requirements were supposedly understood at the beginning of the process, "changing market conditions, and other factors may necessitate changes to requirements" (p. 176). This condition, unfortunately, still applies to the use of Excel as a software package (Mayes & Shank, 2004).

Designing something is not always straight-forward. McConnell (1998) noted that, although the writers block out what the design should look like, the eventual writing of the software code could alter the original plan somewhat with regard to how the system itself handles the various code commands. Thus, when designing the project's architecture, "if detailed design work uncovers flaws in the architecture, the project team revises the architecture using change control procedure." The construction of the code was probably the most continuous portion of the 12 steps. If someone created a systematic architecture, and then created the code based upon it, then there would be a minimum number of issues associated with this particular step in the process. This particular situation can result, due to the fact that the "developer who creates the detailed design for a specific part of the software also writes the code for that part" (p. 176). This is especially true for the use of Excel, if only one person occupies all of the roles involved with the software design project (Ragsdale, 2008).

Part of eventual error testing is supported in the testing step. McConnell (1998) explained that when programmers were coding a particular stage of development, with regard to the lines of code, there should be a "full set of test cases needed to test the functionality developed during the stage." In other words, no administrator or programmer could sign off on the coding, stating that the code was complete, unless a specific module of code had been tested with the associated set of test cases to show that the code module was indeed actually error-free. The user documentation updates should be performed in line with the other construction activities, according to the stage of development, in order to keep pace with the mountain of paperwork that developed during software design and construction. Although, as in the requirements update step, the coders and managers originally knew what was required, conditions during the coding and construction process have changed. That means that the "requirements specification" and "user manual" must also be updated, as the computer code is constructed, in a changed manner, from the original requirements specifications. This actually makes the software development flow easier and more predictably in the long-run, if the team updates the documents as the code is developed, written and tested. In this way, the information is fresh in everyone's mind and an accurate user manual is available to eventually distribute with the completed software package (p. 176). This consideration is probably not so important in Excel, but it can be if the software is to be used externally - in other words, outside of the institution where it was written. Use in the public domain would inherently require a user's manual to make the tenets of the program understandable (Ragsdale, 2008).

In the development cycle associated with software, in this particular case a psychological piece of software to be used as an assessment instrument for career counseling, there is a step that involves a review. McConnell (1998) mentioned that a "technical review" should involve the people who developed a piece of software. Of the two different types of reviews, coding and designing, it would be difficult to determine which type of review would be more important. However, the principals should be involved with both types of review in that both reviews occur after the "post-architecture period," and both types of review generally involve the principals of both teams (who actually worked on the project). The important concept to realize in this part of the discussion is not the obvious statements concerning the fact that both reviews should occur. The important thing to remember is that the overall development plan should allow time to be budgeted for both of these reviews in order to promote the success of the project in totality (p. 177). Although this is a major consideration in software that involves tens of thousands of lines of code, the point is probably moot in an Excel program that only has a few hundred lines of code. It would generally be a situation that is depicted by a program-as-you-go sort of mentality (Brown, 1999).

A continuing step in the overall process is the correction of errors in the program architecture, or in the code itself. McConnell (1998) maintained that a software project should only be allowed to continue to completion with the inherent stipulation that intermediate testing of the various steps or modules of code should occur after each step is completed. In other words, the developers should compel the programmers to make certain that the code was error free at the conclusion of each stage of the process of development, instead of waiting until the end of development to see if the software was functional. It would be important to perform verification at each step of the process, to make certain that the errors exposed by testing were corrected, before the next step of the process was allowed to begin. In this manner, a higher quality of the final product (the piece of software) could be realized by the developers (p. 177). Although this is a major consideration in software that involves tens of thousands of lines of code, the point is probably moot in an Excel program that only has a few hundred lines of code. Again, it would generally be a situation that is depicted by a program-as-you-go sort of mentality (Brown, 1999).

The coordination of any project can be important, but it can be extremely important concerning the development of specialized software. McConnell (1998) directed that if the preceding steps discussed to this point were followed, then the amount of "technical coordination" would be minimized. However, this technical coordination step is a step that should be budgeted, with regard to time allocation in the development cycle, in order to make certain that the project concludes on schedule with enough practically useful code to actually be released. Different groups should meet concerning a project of considerable size. The main concern was that the developers should be available to the coders, who should be available to the technical writers who write the user manuals, who should be available to the administrators to discuss scheduling.

As mentioned in a previous step, the more people who are involved in the overall project, the more the pathways of communication that are eventually involved and the more convoluted the process can become (inviting errors of all types) (p. 177). Although this is a major consideration in software that involves tens of thousands of lines of code, the point is probably moot in an Excel program that only has a few hundred lines of code. This would generally be a situation that is depicted by a program-as-you-go sort of mentality (Brown, 1999).

The software choice summary

There can be a number of risks involved with software development. McConnell (1998) even contended that "stage planning should be risk driven." Administrators should proceed with caution, and review the risk assessment lists, on a periodic basis, to determine if the risks were being adequately addressed and whether those risks were being minimized or even eliminated. As with the other steps that have been mentioned previously, risks change. Risk can evolve as the project evolves, due to a number of factors: requirements updates; design changes; user changes; other considerations not foreseen at the onset of the project (p. 177). Excel usually does not involve this inherent type of risk. With a program-as-you-go mentality, the code writer could easily address this in a few hundred lines of code in just minutes (Brown, 1999).

As with project management fundamentals, there should be some sort of mechanism available to track the progress of the software project's evolution. There are a number of software packages that are commercially available that track tasks and task sub-sets, in addition to Project Management Professional software, that would allow administrators to track the progress of a software project. With Excel, this is intuitively a given due to the simplicity of the coding process.

This particular step may seem to be something of a re-statement of a previous step, but it is actually an independent step unto itself. McConnell (1998) suggested that there should be a step in the development process wherein the software project should be in what's known to be a "releasable state." In other words, the project should be able to stand alone. The piece of software should be able to be combined, from separate modules and pieces of code, for such a release. However, the release should be considered carefully from a business standpoint. Should the release be to the development partners, the end-user, or just other project managers for software evaluation? The list of possibilities might be endless, so this is something that should be a decision in place before the project is started in order to eliminate confusion and unwarranted arguing at the conclusion of the project. An important consideration, regardless to which level the software package is released, is quality coordination. The "quality assurance group" should always get the final edition of the software to look at the parsing, help desk hints and module functions to approve a functional edition for an ultimate release to the end-user or customer (p. 178). Although this a major consideration in software that involves tens of thousands of lines of code, the point is probably moot in an Excel program that only has a few hundred lines of code. This would generally be a situation that is depicted by a program-as-you-go sort of mentality, since the coder occupies essentially all of the traditional positions in the design process (Brown, 1999).

All things eventually conclude, regardless of the eventual outcome of the project. McConnell (1998) concluded that a software project needed an "end-of-stage wrap-up" in order to examine what went well for the project and what didn't. Further, this would be a last chance effort to adjust for any changes to the overall direction of the project. This final step also provided a development tool to save time on future projects, by looking at the steps that went well, and those that didn't, in order to set in place workable frameworks for future projects. If the adage that time is money is still accurate, this wrap-up was a good tool to employ in order to save time and money on future projects by adjusting for the tasks that were poorly accomplished on the present software development project (p. 179). This particular idea does seem to be a good procedural function for any project. But, since the coder is using a program-as-you-go mentality, most of the formality could probably fall by the wayside and a cursory look at the code would be all that's required to have a solidly functional framework base (Mayes & Shank, 2004).

Psychological input for the assessment instrument

Over the years, greater and greater importance has been placed upon one's work in today's marketplace. Yost and Corbishley (1987) suggested that the place of work in most people's lives reveals that career choice has the potential for affecting all aspects of a person's existence. In Western society, work is a major source of status, identity, and gratification...This preoccupation with work is understandable when we consider the time involved and the needs work can meet. In a lifetime the average person spends more time at work than any other single activity except sleep. (pp. 2-3)

Luzzo (2000) maintained that almost one-half of students in colleges were adults, over 25 years of age, and that they were individuals who had worked in the economy and had decided to return to college. Also, universities have graduate students, who are usually older than the general college population, and this further tended to skew the statistics toward the older student demographic (p. 191).

Luzzo (2000) stated that there were economic reasons for these older students to return to a college environment for more training. In fact, "economic factors (e.g. enhancement of career development, expansion of job opportunities" could be some of the main reasons for the students' return to the universities. However, the career counseling system, which does not do a very good job with relation to career placement or counseling assistance required (Tang, Pan, & Newmeyer, 2008; Wolniak & Pascarella, 2007; Patton & Creed, 2007; Bloxom et al, 2008), was actually geared toward the younger students who were transitioning from high school to college (p. 191).

Bloom and Peters (1961) noted, with regard to a scaling procedure, that concerning specific situations, such as the high school to college transition populations of students, that the application of a "scaling procedure" does make a considerable difference in the positive correlation indices of potential grades concerning these types of students. By such procedural usage, the positive correlations were in the ranges of +.68 to +.77, an extraordinarily high positive correlation, statistically. Thus, the proper scale for personality profiles of these students, in such a transition, does have a considerable impact upon the career counselor's work with the client base, with regard to the counseling of the high school to college transition populations of students (p. 74).

Bryon (2006) contended that the construction of psychometric profiles, for extensive use in the career counseling of transitional students, encompassed a variety of considerations. For example, some of the tenets of such tests, for accuracy to be covered were: "Numerical Reasoning," as demonstrated by "key operations or sequencing" (p. 79); "Personality Questionnaires," as demonstrated by "communicating...planning...resources management...motivation...ideal role...risk attitudes... success mindset" (p. 114); and "Non-Verbal Reasoning, Mechanical Comprehension and IQ Tests," as demonstrated by individual test batteries in each of the preceding categories. The researcher felt that the only way to develop adequate psychometrics was to have these answers to the test batteries, so that the client could be "pigeonholed" into a particular specialty (for pursuit of academic study) (p. 124).

Oldham and Morris (1995) found that "where you've come from and where you're headed" were inter-related (p. 385). Further, "you are who you are by the time you exit your childhood - yet experience and biology continually mold and modify you, building on what has gone before and sometimes pointing you in new directions" (p. 397). This represents the conglomeration of the antiquated nature vs. nurture psychological argument. However, this is important with relevance to the psychology of career counseling as supported by a number of researchers from the Depth segment of this paper (Tang, Pan, & Newmeyer, 2008; Wolniak & Pascarella, 2007; Patton & Creed, 2007; Bloxom et al, 2008).

Janda (2001) indicated that there are a variety of test batteries that already existed, but were simply not being used in the transitional population. For example, such tests already encompass: "The Automatic Thoughts Questionnaire" (p. 32); "The Personal Behavior Inventory" (p. 38); "The Survey of Personal Beliefs" (p. 44); "The Barratt Impulsiveness Scale" (p. 54); "The Multidimensional Body-Self Relations Questionnaire" (p. 62); "The Self-Esteem Rating Scale" (p. 14); "The Adult Self-Expression Scale" (p. 90); "The Self-Efficacy Scale" (p. 154); and "The Thriving Scale" (p 168). Since these examinations and tests already exist, but for some reason have not been utilized in the career assessment, transition and counseling of high school to college student populations (Harrington & Harrington, 2007; Larson & Borgen, 2006), my contention is that these standardized tests should be used in an Excel computer software assessment tool and administered/assessed in these student populations for the actual counseling of clients.

The evaluation of such a computer assessment instrument would only logically be involved after the implementation/deployment of such an instrument. However, this discussion is a conservative discussion of some of the more conservative ideas associated with a theoretical construct of such a career counseling, assessment instrument. It is acknowledged that such an assessment of the instrument could only occur (in reality) if the instrument were to be actually constructed and utilized in these populations of students. Intuitively, the writer believes that such an instrument would have extraordinarily high value for the career counseling of the student transition populations examined in this paper. However, with regard to the reality of space and time requirements for any paper, it is an acknowledged reality that the actual correlations and value of such a theoretical assessment instrument would be derived from its actual, eventual construction and deployment. After years of practical usage, a further study could be performed to determine the value and usefulness, with regard to these populations, of such an instrument. Further study is needed in this area and it is left for future researchers to use the combined information presented herein to actually design and deploy such an assessment instrument.

Summary

A discussion of the knowledge requirements, necessary to undertake the programming of a psychological test instrument for practical use in career counseling of the prospective college students in transition to a junior college or work college institution, must first mention the prerequisite items, that form a framework for discussion. These items, of the more pertinent areas that might be addressed in the framework for such a discussion, were addressed herein above.

A proposed solution to dichotomous observations, concerning the programming of software to meet particular needs, was the published results in the late 1980's, that described a particular difference between the essentials necessary to engineer software and the transient technical aspects associated with the use of a particular software coding language that would quickly, in just a few short years, become obsolete. An *essential* property was something that made something, by definition, to be what it was. Although the technical aspects became obsolete in only a few short years, it was the tenets of the *accidental* properties (concerning computing and software design), that actually made computer work possible at all. It was these *accidental* properties of software and engineering knowledge that overcame the mercurial nature of the *essential* properties. Thus, McConnell (2004b) stated that considerable improvement had already been made with regard to the *accidental* parts of programming. The real work to be done remained, however, in improving the previously discussed essential elements of the framework known as, "*complexity, conformity, changeability, and invisibility*" (p. 39).

The more communication paths you have, the more time you spend communicating and the more opportunities are created for communication mistakes. Concerning the time allocated and allotted to the actual steps of the project, the size of the project, with regard to the number of lines of computer code, had a dramatic influence upon how much time was spent on each step of the development activities. McConnell (2004a) realized that on a smaller project, one in the range of 8,000 to 10,000 lines of computer code, about two-thirds of the overall time spent on the project was spent upon construction of the software program. Only about five percent of the total time allocated was actually spent on preliminary planning aspects associated with "architecture and requirements" (pp. 654-655).

A software project, regardless of the size considerations, must have a logical order of steps to be followed so that it will eventually become complete. McConnell (1998) detailed a variety of considerations, and all one dozen of those considerations played an important role in our prospective piece of psychological and career counseling software's theoretical completion. McConnell detailed those steps and, in order to promote success of the software project, they should be followed and completed in the appropriate order. The twelve steps are, "Requirements updates; Detailed design; Construction; Test case creation; User documentation updates; Technical reviews; Defect corrections; Technical coordination; Risk management; Project tracking; Integration and release; and End-of-stage wrap-up" (p 175).

There can be a number of risks involved with software development. McConnell (1998) even contended that "stage planning should be risk driven." Administrators should proceed with caution, and review the risk assessment lists, on a periodic basis, to determine if the risks were being adequately addressed and whether those risks were being minimized or even eliminated. As with the other steps that have been mentioned previously, risks change. Risk can evolve as the project evolves, due to a number of factors: requirements updates; design changes; user changes; other considerations not foreseen at the onset of the project (p. 177). Excel usually does not involve this inherent type of risk. With a program-as-you-go mentality, the code writer could easily address this in a few hundred lines of code in just minutes (Brown, 1999).

All things eventually conclude, regardless of the eventual outcome of the project. McConnell (1998) concluded that a software project needed an "end-of-stage wrap-up" in order to examine what went well for the project and what didn't. Further, this would be a last chance effort to adjust for any changes to the overall direction of the project. This final step also provided a development tool to save time on future projects, by looking at the steps that went well, and those that didn't, in order to set in place workable frameworks for future projects. If the adage that time is money is still accurate, this wrap-up was a good tool to employ in order to save time and money on future projects by adjusting for those tasks that were poorly accomplished on the present software development project (p. 179). This particular idea seemed to be a good procedural function for any project. But, since the coder is using a program-as-you-go mentality, most of the formality could probably fall by the wayside and a cursory look at the code would be all that's required to have a solidly functional framework base (Mayes & Shank, 2004).

Bryon (2006) contended that the construction of psychometric profiles, for extensive use in the career counseling of transitional students, encompassed a variety of considerations. For example, some of the tenets of such tests, for accuracy to be covered were: "Numerical Reasoning," as demonstrated by "key operations or sequencing" (p. 79); "Personality Questionnaires," as demonstrated by "communicating...planning... resources management...motivation...ideal role...risk attitudes...success mindset" (p. 114); and Non-Verbal Reasoning, Mechanical Comprehension and IQ Tests," as demonstrated by individual test batteries in each of the preceding categories. The researcher felt that the only way to develop adequate psychometrics was to have these answers to the test batteries, so that the client could be "pigeon-holed" into a particular specialty (for the pursuit of academic study) (p. 124).

Oldham and Morris (1995) found that "where you've come from and where you're headed" were inter-related (p. 385). Further, "you are who you are by the time you exit your childhood - yet experience and biology continually mold and modify you, building on what has gone before and sometimes pointing you in new directions" (p. 397). This represented the conglomeration of the antiquated nature vs. nurture psychological argument. However, this is important with relevance to the psychology of career counseling as supported by a number of researchers from the depth segment of this paper (Tang, Pan, & Newmeyer, 2008; Wolniak & Pascarella, 2007; Patton & Creed, 2007; Bloxom et al, 2008).

Janda (2001) indicated that there were a variety of test batteries that already existed, but were simply not being used in the transitional population. For example, such tests already encompass: "The Automatic Thoughts Questionnaire" (p. 32); "The Personal Behavior Inventory" (p. 38); "The Survey of Personal Beliefs" (p. 44); "The Barratt Impulsiveness Scale" (p. 54); "The Multidimensional Body-Self Relations Questionnaire" (p. 62); "The Self-Esteem Rating Scale" (p. 14); "The Adult Self-Expression Scale" (p. 90); "The Self-Efficacy Scale" (p. 154); and "The Thriving Scale" (p 168). Miller (2007) evaluated and compared the findings of a traditional assessment tool (paper), with respect to career planning, to the results derived from an online self-assessment career planning exercise in order to determine the relationships between the two. Since there was a high correlation between the two, simply take the traditional paper assessments depicted above and program them into an Excel spreadsheet software program. Since these examinations and tests already exist, but for some reason have not been utilized in the career assessment, transition and counseling of high school to college student populations (Harrington & Harrington, 2007; Larson & Borgen, 2006), my contention is that these standardized tests should be used in an Excel computer software assessment tool and administered/assessed in these student populations for the actual counseling of clients.

The evaluation of such a computer assessment instrument would be involved after the implementation/ deployment of such an instrument. However, this discussion is a conservative discussion of some of the more conservative ideas associated with a theoretical construct of such a career counseling assessment instrument. It is acknowledged that such an assessment could only occur (in reality) if the instrument were to be constructed and utilized in these populations of students. Intuitively, the writer believes that such an instrument would have extraordinarily high value for the career counseling of the student transition populations examined in this paper. However, with regard to the reality of space and time requirements for any paper, it is an acknowledged reality that the actual correlations and value of such a theoretical assessment instrument would only be derived from its actual, eventual construction and deployment among the student populations addressed herein above. After years of practical usage, a further study could be performed to determine the career counseling assessment instrument's value and usefulness, with regard to the student populations addressed herein above. Further study is needed in this area and it is left for future researchers to use the combined information presented herein to actually design and deploy such a career counseling assessment instrument.

REFERENCES

Amir, T., & Gati, I. (2006). Facets of career decision-making difficulties. *British Journal of Guidance & Counselling, 34*(4), 483-503.

Betz, N., & Wolfe, J. (2005). Measuring confidence for basic domains of vocational activity in high school students. *Journal of Career Assessment, 13*(3), 251-270.

Bloom, B., & Peters, F. (1961). *The use of academic prediction scales.* New York: Crowell-Collier Publishing Co.

Bloxom, J., Bernes, K., Magnusson, K., Gunn, T., Bardick, A., Orr, D., et al. (2008). Grade 12 student career needs and perceptions of the effectiveness of career development services within high schools. *Canadian Journal of Counselling, 42*(2), 79-100.

Blustein, D., Kenna, A., Gill, N., & Devoy, J. (2008). The psychology of working: A new framework for counseling practice and public policy. *The Career Development Quarterly, 56*(2), 294-308.

Brown, J. (1999). *Quick course in Microsoft Excel*. Redmond, WA: Microsoft Press.

Bryon, M. (2006). *The ultimate psychometric test book*. Glasgow: Bell & Bain, Ltd.

Duffy, R., & Sedlacek, W. (2007). The work values of first-year college students: Exploring group differences. *The Career Development Quarterly, 55*(2), 359-364.

Fouad, N., Chen, Y., Guillen, A., Henry, C., Kantemneni, N., Novacovic, A., Priester, P., & Terry, S. (2007). Role induction in career counseling. *The Career Development Quarterly, 56*(3), 19-33.

Ganske, K., & Ashby, J. (2007). Perfectionism and career decision-making self-efficacy. *Journal of Employment Counseling, 44*(1), 17-28.

Harrington, T., & Harrington, J. (2007). Every one has abilities, but do counselors know how to assess all abilities and use this information? *Career Planning & Adult Development Journal, 23*(2), 22-29.

Hull, C. (1943). *Principles of behavior*. New York: Appleton-Century-Crofts.

Janda, L. (2001). *The psychologist's book of personality tests*. New York: John Wiley & Sons, Inc.

Larson, L., & Borgen, F. (2006). Do personality traits contribute to vocational self-efficacy? *Journal of Career Assessment, 14*(3), 295-311.

Luzzo, D. (Ed.). (2000). *Career counseling of college students.* Baltimore, MD: United Book Press.

Mayes, T., & Shank, T. (2004). *Financial analysis.* Mason, OH: Thomson, South-Western.

McConnell, S. (2004a). *Code complete* (2nd ed.). Redmond, WA: Microsoft Press.

McConnell, S. (2004b). *Professional software development.* Boston: Pearson Education, Inc.

McConnell, S. (1998). *Software project survival guide.* Redmond, WA: Microsoft Press.

Miller, M. (2007). Examining the degree of congruency between a traditional career instrument and an online self-assessment exercise. *Journal of Employment Counseling, 44*(3), 11-16.

Moore, R., Moore, M., Grimes, P., Millea, M., Lehman, M., & Pearson, A., et al. (2007). Developing an intervention bridging program for at-risk students before the traditional pre-freshman summer program. *College Student Journal, 41*(1), 151-159.

Nauta, M. (2007). Career interests, self-efficacy, and personality as antecedents of career exploration. *Journal of Career Assessment, 15*(2), 162-180.

Oldham, J., & Morris, L. (1995). *The new personality self-portrait.* New York: Bantam Books.

Patton, W., & Creed, P. (2007). Occupational aspirations and expectations of Australian adolescents. *Australian Journal of Career Development, 16*(1), 46-59.

Ragsdale, C. (2008). *Spreadsheet modeling & decision analysis* (5th ed.). Canada: Louiseville Gagne Canada.

Skinner, B. (1974). *About behaviorism.* New York: Knopf.

Smith, S., & Guthrie, E. (1921). *General psychology in terms of behavior.* New York: Kessinger Publishing Company.

Spiegel, M. (1999). *Mathematical handbook of formulas and tables.* New York: McGraw-Hill.

Spiegel, M., Schiller, J., & Srinivasan, R. (2000). *Probability and statistics* (2nd ed.). New York: McGraw-Hill.

Tang, M., Pan, W., & Newmeyer, M. (2008). Factors influencing high school students' career aspirations. *Professional School Counseling, 11*(5), 285-295.

Thorndike, E. (1932, 1971). *The fundamentals of learning.* New York: AMS Press.

Watson, J. (1924). *Behaviourism.* New York: W. W. Norton & Co., Inc.

Wolniak, G., & Pascarella, E. (2007). Initial evidence on the long-term impacts of work colleges. *Research in Higher Education, 48*(1), 39-71.

Yost, E., & Corbishley, M. (1987). *Career counseling.* San Francisco: Jossey-Bass Publishers.